BIG BOOK OF
Crochet
ACCESSORIES

LEISURE ARTS, INC. • Maumelle, Arkansas

Contents

Accessorize your life from head (with hats & headbands) to toe (socks & boot cuffs) all year long with our biggest collection of crochet accessories! Choose from 46 colorful projects that are fun to make, give & wear!

Delicate earrings, necklaces, & bracelets dress up your wardrobe while showcasing your talent. With all the thread colors available, it's easy to coordinate your jewelry with your OOTD.

Hats, scarves, caps, shrugs, shawls, bags, totes, socks, backpacks, ear warmers, mitts,& cowls are all presented in easy-to-follow instructions.

And let's not forget your family & friends—hats, scarves, gloves—crochet up quickly for that last minute gift.

You can also practice new techniques, such as fair isle crochet, crocheted cables, & the heavily textured crocodile stitch. It's easy to master these techniques on a smaller scale project.

DESIGNED BY
Kristi Simpson

Grace

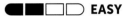 **EASY**

Finished Measurements:

15½" x 62½" (39.5 cm x 159 cm)

SHOPPING LIST

- **Yarn** (Light Weight)
  [3.5 ounces, 306 yards
  (100 grams, 280 meters) per skein]:
  - 3 skeins

- **Crochet Hook**
  - Size J (6 mm) **or** size needed for gauge

- **Additional Supplies**
  - Split-ring marker

Gauge Information:

13 dc and 8 rows = 4" (10 cm)

Gauge Swatch:

4" (10 cm) square

Ch 15.

Row 1: Dc in fourth ch from hook **(3 skipped chs count as first dc)** and in each ch across: 13 dc.

Rows 2-8: Ch 3 **(counts as first dc)**, turn; dc in next dc and in each dc across.

Finish off.

Body is worked across the length of the wrap.

BODY

Ch 205.

Row 1 (Right side): Working in back ridge of chs *(Fig. 2, page 155)*, dc in fourth ch from hook **(3 skipped chs count as first dc)** and in each ch across to last 20 chs, ★ ch 1, skip next ch, dc in next ch; repeat from ★ across: 193 dc and 10 chs (203 sts).

Row 2: Ch 4 **(counts as first dc plus ch 1, now and throughout)**, turn; skip next ch, dc in next dc, ★ ch 1, skip next st, dc in next dc; repeat from ★ 18 times **more**, dc in next 20 dc, place marker around last dc made for st placement, dc in next dc and in each dc across: 183 dc and 20 chs.

Row 3: Ch 3 **(counts as first dc, now and throughout)**, turn; dc in next dc and in each dc across ending in marked dc (remove marker), ★ ch 1, skip next st, dc in next dc; repeat from ★ across: 173 dc and 30 chs.

Row 4: Ch 4, turn; skip next ch, dc in next dc, ★ ch 1, skip next st, dc in next dc; repeat from ★ 38 times **more**, dc in next 20 dc, place marker around last dc made, dc in next dc and in each dc across: 163 dc and 40 chs.

Row 5: Ch 3, turn; dc in next dc and in each dc across ending in marked dc (remove marker), ★ ch 1, skip next st, dc in next dc; repeat from ★ across: 153 dc and 50 chs.

Row 6: Ch 4, turn; skip next ch, dc in next dc, ★ ch 1, skip next st, dc in next dc; repeat from ★ 58 times **more**, dc in next 20 dc, place marker around last dc made, dc in next dc and in each dc across: 143 dc and 60 chs.

Row 7: Ch 3, turn; dc in next dc and in each dc across ending in marked dc (remove marker), ★ ch 1, skip next st, dc in next dc; repeat from ★ across: 133 dc and 70 chs.

Row 8: Ch 4, turn; skip next ch, dc in next dc, ★ ch 1, skip next st, dc in next dc; repeat from ★ 78 times **more**, dc in next 20 dc, place marker around last dc made for st placement, dc in next dc and in each dc across: 123 dc and 80 chs.

Row 9: Ch 3, turn; dc in next dc and in each dc across ending in marked dc (remove marker), ★ ch 1, skip next st, dc in next dc; repeat from ★ across: 113 dc and 90 chs.

Rows 10 and 11: Ch 4, turn; skip next st, dc in next dc, ★ ch 1, skip next st, dc in next dc; repeat from ★ across: 102 dc and 101 chs.

Row 12: Ch 3, turn; (dc in next ch-1 sp, dc in next dc) 10 times, (ch 1, skip next ch, dc in next dc) 10 times, place marker around last dc made, (ch 1, skip next ch, dc in next dc) across: 112 dc and 91 chs.

Row 13: Ch 4, turn; skip next ch, dc in next dc, ★ ch 1, skip next ch, dc in next dc; repeat from ★ across ending in marked dc (remove marker), (dc in next ch-1 sp, dc in next dc) 10 times, dc in next dc and in each dc across: 122 dc and 81 chs.

Row 14: Ch 3, turn; dc in next dc and in each dc across to next ch-1 sp, (dc in next ch-1 sp, dc in next dc) 10 times, (ch 1, skip next ch, dc in next dc) 10 times, place marker around last dc made, (ch 1, skip next ch, dc in next dc) across: 132 dc and 71 chs.

Rows 15-19: Repeat Rows 13 and 14 twice, then repeat Row 13 once **more**: 182 dc and 21 chs.

Row 20: Ch 4, turn; skip next dc, dc in next dc, ★ ch 1, skip next dc, dc in next dc; repeat from ★ 8 times **more**, dc in next 20 dc, place marker around last dc made for st placement, dc in next dc and in each dc across to next ch-1 sp, (dc in next ch-1 sp, dc in next dc) 10 times, (ch 1, skip next ch, dc in next dc) across.

Row 21: Ch 3, turn; (dc in next ch-1 sp, dc in next dc) 11 times, dc in next dc and in each dc across ending in marked dc (remove marker), (ch 1, skip next st, dc in next dc) across: 183 dc and 20 chs.

Row 22: Ch 4, turn; skip next ch, dc in next dc, ★ ch 1, skip next st, dc in next dc; repeat from ★ 28 times **more**, dc in next 20 dc, place marker around last dc made, dc in next dc and in each dc across: 173 dc and 30 chs.

Row 23: Ch 3, turn; dc in next dc and in each dc across ending in marked dc (remove marker), ★ ch 1, skip next st, dc in next dc; repeat from ★ across: 163 dc and 40 chs.

Row 24: Ch 4, turn; skip next ch, dc in next dc, ★ ch 1, skip next st, dc in next dc; repeat from ★ 48 times **more**, dc in next 20 dc, place marker around last dc made, dc in next dc and in each dc across: 153 dc and 50 chs.

Row 25: Ch 3, turn; dc in next dc and in each dc across ending in marked dc (remove marker), ★ ch 1, skip next st, dc in next dc; repeat from ★ across: 143 dc and 60 chs.

Row 26: Ch 4, turn; skip next ch, dc in next dc, ★ ch 1, skip next st, dc in next dc; repeat from ★ 68 times **more**, dc in next 20 dc, place marker around last dc made, dc in next dc and in each dc across: 133 dc and 70 chs.

Row 27: Ch 3, turn; dc in next dc and in each dc across ending in marked dc (remove marker), ★ ch 1, skip next st, dc in next dc; repeat from ★ across: 123 dc and 80 chs.

Row 28: Ch 4, turn; skip next st, dc in next dc, ★ ch 1, skip next st, dc in next dc; repeat from ★ 88 times **more**, dc in next dc and in each dc across: 113 dc and 90 chs.

Row 29: Ch 4, turn; skip next st, dc in next dc, ★ ch 1, skip next st, dc in next dc; repeat from ★ across: 102 dc and 101 chs.

Row 30: Ch 6, turn; slip st in first dc and in next ch, ★ ch 6, slip st in next dc and in next ch; repeat from ★ across to last dc, ch 6, slip st in last dc; finish off.

DESIGNED BY
Melissa Leapman

Fair Isle Set

 **INTERMEDIATE**

Finished Measurements:

Scarf: 7½" wide x 62½" long (19 cm x 159 cm)
Hat: Fits head circumference 20" (51 cm)

SHOPPING LIST

- **Yarn** (Medium Weight) **4** MEDIUM
  [3.5 ounces, 210 yards
  (100 grams, 192 meters) per skein]:

  ### Scarf
  - Color A (Grey) - 3 skeins
  - Color B (Black) - 2 skeins
  - Color C (Aran) - 1 skein
  - Color D (Lt Red) - 1 skein
  - Color E (Red) - 1 skein
  - Color F (Dk Red) - 1 skein

  ### Hat
  - Color A (Grey) - 1 skein
  - Color B (Black) - 1 skein
  - Color C (Aran) - 1 skein
  - Color D (Lt Red) - 1 skein
  - Color E (Red) - 1 skein
  - Color F (Dk Red) - 1 skein

- **Crochet Hook**
  - Size I (5.5 mm) **or** size needed
    for gauge

- **Additional Supplies**
  - Yarn needle (for Hat)

Gauge Information:

In Fair Isle pattern,
16 sc and 14 rnds = 4" (10 cm)

Gauge Swatch:

3" wide (flattened) x 2"high
(7.5 cm x 5 cm)

With Black, ch 24.

Work same as Scarf, page 12,
for 7 rnds: 24 sc.

Finish off.

STITCH GUIDE

SINGLE CROCHET 2 TOGETHER
(abbreviated sc2tog)

Pull up a loop in each of next 2 sc, YO and draw through all 3 loops on hook **(counts as one sc)**.

Before beginning your project, read through the Fair Isle section of the General Instructions **(pages 157 & 158)**.

SCARF

With Color B, ch 60; being careful **not** to twist ch, join with slip st to back ridge of first ch to form a ring **(Fig. 2, page 155)**.

Rnd 1 (Right side)**:** Ch 1, sc in back ridge of same st as joining and each ch around; join with slip st to first sc: 60 sc.

The **right** side will always be facing you. When changing colors, drop yarn to **back** of work; do **not** cut yarn.

Rnd 2: Ch 1, sc in Back Loop Only of same st as joining and each sc around **(Fig. 4, page 155)**; join with slip st to first sc.

Only two colors are used per round. Change colors **(Figs. 11a-e, page 157)** carrying the unused color **loosely** on the inside of the Scarf and working over the floats on subsequent rounds **(Figs. 11f & g, pages 157 & 158)**. Yarn can be carried up 2 rounds. Cut yarns when they are no longer needed.

Rnd 3: Ch 1, working in Back Loops Only, sc in same st as joining and in next sc, sc in next sc changing to Color C, ★ sc in next sc changing to Color B, sc in next 2 sc, sc in next sc changing to Color C; repeat from ★ around to last sc, sc in last sc; join with slip st to first sc.

Rnds 4-18: Ch 1, sc in Back Loop Only of same st as joining and each sc around following Chart Rnds 4-18 **(see How to Follow a Chart, page 158)**; join with slip st to first sc.

Repeat Rnds 2-18 until Scarf measures approximately 62" (157.5 cm) from beginning ch, ending by working Rnd 7.

Finish off.

Trim: Flatten Scarf with joining at center back. With front facing and working through **both** loops of each sc on **both** layers, join Color B with sc in first st at fold on last row **(see Joining With Sc, page 154)**; sc in next st and in each st across; finish off.

Repeat across bottom edge.

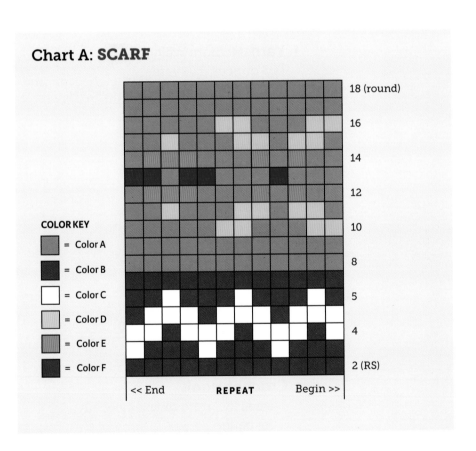

Chart A: SCARF

COLOR KEY
- = Color A
- = Color B
- = Color C
- = Color D
- = Color E
- = Color F

<< End   REPEAT   Begin >>

On all rounds, follow **Chart A** from **right** to **left**.

Tassel *(Make 4)*

Cut a piece of cardboard 3" wide x 5" long (7.5 cm x 12.5 cm). Wind a double strand of each color of yarn around the cardboard twice. Cut an 18" (45.5 cm) length of Color B and insert it under all of the strands at the top of the cardboard; pull up **tightly** and tie securely. Leave the yarn ends long enough to attach the tassel. Cut the yarn at the opposite end of the cardboard *(Fig. A)* and then remove it. Cut a 6" (15 cm) length of Color A and wrap it **tightly** around the tassel twice, 1" (2.5 cm) below the top *(Fig. B)*; tie securely. Trim ends.

Attach one Tassel to each corner of Scarf.

Fig. A

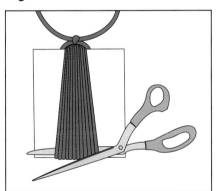

Fig. B

HAT

Ribbing

With Color A, ch 8.

Row 1 (Right side)**:** Sc in back ridge of second ch from hook and each ch across *(Fig. 2, page 155)*: 7 sc.

Note: Loop a short piece of yarn around any stitch to mark Row 1 as **right** side.

Row 2: Ch 1, turn; sc in Back Loop Only of each sc across *(Fig. 4, page 155)*.

Repeat Row 2 until Ribbing measures approximately 20" (51 cm) from beginning ch when slightly stretched, ending by working a **right** side row.

Joining Row: Ch 1, turn; hold beginning ch and last row with **right** side together and working through **inside** loops of each st on **both** layers, slip st in each st across; finish off.

Turn Ribbing **right** side out.

Body

> The **right** side will always be facing you. When changing colors, drop yarn to **back** of work; do **not** cut yarn.

Rnd 1 (Right side)**:** With **right** side facing, join Color B with sc in seam *(see Joining With Sc, page 154)*; work 83 sc evenly spaced along end of rows; join with slip st to first sc: 84 sc.

Rnd 2: Ch 1, sc in Back Loop Only of same st as joining and each sc around; join with slip st to first sc.

Only two colors are used per round. Change colors *(Figs. 11a-e, page 157)* carrying the unused color **loosely** on the **back** of the Hat and working over the floats on subsequent rounds *(Figs. 11f & g, pages 157 & 158)*. Yarn can be carried up 2 rounds. Cut yarns when they are no longer needed.

Rnd 3: Ch 1, working in Back Loops Only, sc in same st as joining and in next sc, sc in next sc changing to Color C, ★ sc in next sc changing to Color B, sc in next 2 sc, sc in next sc changing to Color C; repeat from ★ around to last sc, sc in last sc; join with slip st to first sc.

13

Rnds 4-24: Ch 1, sc in Back Loop Only of same st as joining and each sc around following Chart Rnds 4-24 *(see How to Follow a Chart, page 158)*; join with slip st to first sc.

Finish off.

Crown

Continue to work in Back Loops Only throughout.

Rnd 1: With **right** side facing, join Color A with sc in same st as joining; sc in next sc and in each sc around; join with slip st to first sc.

Rnd 2: Ch 1, beginning in same st as joining, (sc2tog, sc in next 5 sc) around; join with slip st to first sc: 72 sc.

Rnd 3: Ch 1, beginning in same st as joining, (sc2tog, sc in next 4 sc) around; join with slip st to first sc: 60 sc.

Rnd 4: Ch 1, beginning in same st as joining, (sc2tog, sc in next 3 sc) around; join with slip st to first sc: 48 sc.

Rnd 5: Ch 1, beginning in same st as joining, (sc2tog, sc in next 2 sc) around; join with slip st to first sc: 36 sc.

Rnds 6 and 7: Ch 1, beginning in same st as joining, (sc2tog, sc in next sc) around; join with slip st to first sc: 16 sc.

Rnd 8: Ch 1, beginning in same st as joining, sc2tog around; join with slip st to first sc, finish off leaving a long end for sewing: 8 sc.

Thread yarn needle with long end and weave needle through sts on Rnd 8 *(Fig. 8, page 156)*; pull **tightly** to close and secure end.

Chart B: **HAT**

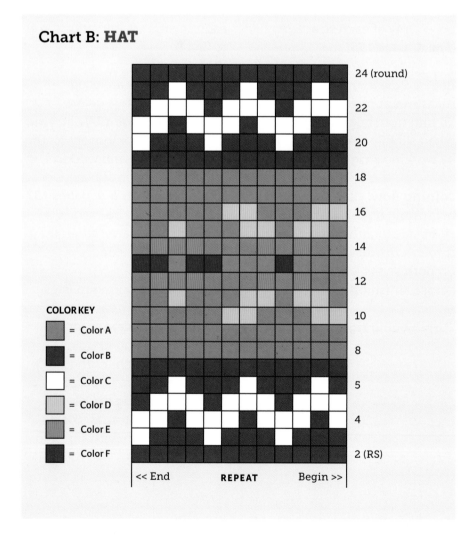

On all rounds, follow **Chart B** from **right** to **left**.

Mandala Bag

 **EASY**

DESIGNED BY
Kristi Simpson

Finished Measurements:

22¾" circumference x 10¼" high x 2½" deep (58 cm x 26 cm x6.5 cm) (excluding Strap)

SHOPPING LIST

- **Yarn** (Medium Weight) 4
  [4 ounces, 203 yards
  (113 grams, 186 meters) per skein]:
  - Off White - 2 skeins
  - Orange - 17 yards (15.5 meters)
  - Dk Pink - 12 yards (11 meters)
  - Peach - 11 yards (10 meters)
  - Brick - 8 yards (7.5 meters)
  - Yellow - small amount

- **Crochet Hook**
  - Size H (5 mm) **or** size needed for gauge

- **Additional Supplies**
  - Yarn needle

Gauge Information:

14 sc and 16 rows/rnds = 4" (10 cm)

Gauge Swatch:
4" (10 cm) square

With Off White, ch 15.

Row 1: Sc in second ch from hook and in each ch across: 14 sc.

Rows 2-16: Ch 1, turn; sc in each sc across.

Finish off.

STITCH GUIDE

SINGLE CROCHET 2 TOGETHER
(abbreviated sc2tog)

Pull up a loop in each of next 2 sc, YO and draw through all 3 loops on hook **(counts as one sc)**.

BASE

With Off White, ch 31.

Row 1: Sc in second ch from hook and in each ch across: 30 sc.

Rows 2-10: Ch 1, turn; sc in each sc across.

BODY

Rnd 1 (Right side): Ch 1, sc in end of each row across; sc in free loops of each ch across *(Fig. 3b, page 155)*; sc in end of each row across; sc in each sc across Row 10; join with slip st to first sc: 80 sc.

Note: Loop a short piece of yarn around any stitch to mark Rnd 1 as **right** side.

Rnd 2: Ch 1, hdc in same st as joining and in each sc around; do **not** join, place a marker to indicate the beginning of the rnd *(see Markers, page 154)*.

Rnds 3-36: Sc in each st around.

Rnd 37: (Sc2tog, sc in next 8 sc) around: 72 sc.

Rnd 38: (Sc2tog, sc in next 7 sc) around: 64 sc.

Rnds 39 and 40: Sc in each sc around; at end of Rnd 40, slip st in next sc, finish off.

STRAP

Row 1: With right **side** facing, join Off White with sc in seventh sc after joining slip st *(see Joining With Sc, page 154)*; sc in next 9 sts, leave remaining sts unworked: 10 sc.

Rows 2-64: Ch 1, turn; sc in each sc across.

Finish off leaving a long end for sewing.

Skip next 22 sc on Rnd 40 of Body and, being careful **not** to twist, sew sc on Row 64 to next 10 sts.

Using Off White, sew end of Rows 11-55 together.

MANDALA

Rnd 1 (Right side)**:** With Yellow, ch 2; 9 sc in second ch from hook; join with slip st to first sc.

Note: Mark Rnd 1 as **right** side.

Rnd 2: Ch 1, sc in same st as joining, ch 3, (sc in next sc, ch 3) around; join with slip st to first sc, finish off: 9 ch-3 sps.

Rnd 3: With **right** side facing, join Peach with slip st in any ch-3 sp; ch 2, YO, insert hook in **same** sp, YO and pull up a loop, YO and draw through 2 loops on hook, YO, insert hook in **next** ch-3 sp, YO and pull up a loop, YO and draw through 2 loops on hook, YO, insert hook in same sp, YO and pull up a loop, YO and draw through 2 loops on hook, YO and draw through all 4 loops on hook, ch 7, ★ **†** [YO, insert hook in **same** sp, YO and pull up a loop, YO and draw through 2 loops on hook] twice (3 loops on hook) **†**, YO, insert hook in **next** ch-3 sp, YO and pull up a loop, YO and draw through 2 loops on hook, YO, insert hook in **same** sp, YO and pull up a loop, YO and draw through 2 loops on hook, YO and draw through all 5 loops on hook, ch 7; repeat from ★ 6 times **more**, then repeat from **†** to **†** once, [YO, insert hook in **same** sp as joining, YO and pull up a loop, YO and draw through 2 loops on hook] twice, YO and draw through all 5 loops on hook, ch 7; join with slip st to first st.

Rnd 4: Slip st in next ch-7 sp, ch 1, (sc, ch 5) twice in same sp and in each ch-7 sp around; join with slip st to first sc, finish off: 18 ch-5 sps.

Rnd 5: With **right** side facing, join Dk Pink with sc in last ch-5 sp made; ch 1, (dc, ch 1) 7 times in next ch-5 sp, ★ sc in next ch-5 sp, ch 1, (dc, ch 1) 7 times in next ch-5 sp; repeat from ★ around; join with slip st to first sc, finish off: 72 sts and 72 ch-1 sps.

Rnd 6: With **right** side facing, join Orange with sc in center dc of any 7-dc group; ch 5, skip next 2 ch-1 sps, sc in next dc, ch 5, skip next 4 ch-1 sps, sc in next dc, ★ (ch 5, skip next 2 ch-1 sps, sc in next dc) twice, ch 5, skip next 4 ch-1 sps, sc in next dc; repeat from ★ around to last 2 ch-1 sps, ch 2, dc in first sc to form last ch-5 sp: 27 ch-5 sps.

Rnd 7: Ch 1, sc in last ch-5 sp made, ch 6, sc in next ch-5 sp, ch 1, (dc, ch 1) 5 times in next ch-5 sp, ★ sc in next ch-5 sp, ch 6, sc in next ch-5 sp, ch 1, (dc, ch 1) 5 times in next ch-5 sp; repeat from ★ around; join with slip st to first sc, finish off: 63 sts and 63 sps.

Rnd 8: With **right** side facing, join Brick with sc in any ch-6 sp; (sc, ch 3, 2 sc) in same sp, ch 3, skip next 2 ch-1 sps, sc in next dc and in next ch-1 sp, (slip st, ch 3, slip st) in next dc, sc in next ch-1 sp and in next dc, ch 3, skip next 2 ch-1 sps, ★ (2 sc, ch 3, 2 sc) in next ch-6 sp, ch 3, skip next 2 ch-1 sps, sc in next dc and in next ch-1 sp, (slip st, ch 3, slip st) in next dc, sc in next ch-1 sp and in next dc, ch 3, skip next 2 ch-1 sps; repeat from ★ around; join with slip st to first sc, finish off leaving a long end for sewing.

Using photo as a guide for placement, sew wrong side of Mandala to right side of Body.

DESIGNED BY
Becky Stevens

Lattice Set

 **INTERMEDIATE**

Finished Measurements:

Scarf: 5½{6¾}" wide x 50{60}" high [14{17} cm x 127{152.5} cm]

Hat: Fits 17{20}"/43{51} cm head circumference

Size Note: We have printed the instructions for the sizes in different colors to make it easier for you to find:

Child size = BLUE
Adult size = PINK
Both sizes = BLACK

Gauge Information:

Child: 5½"w x 4¾"h (14 cm x 12 cm)

Work same as Scarf, page 22, for 18 rows: 24 sts.

Adult: 6¾"w x 4¼"h (17 cm x 10.75 cm)

Work same as Scarf, page 22, for 14 rows: 24 sts.

SHOPPING LIST

- **Yarn** (Medium Weight)

Complete Set

Child

[6 ounces, 315 yards (170 grams, 288 meters) per skein]:
- 2 skeins

Adult

[7 ounces, 364 yards (198 grams, 333 meters) per skein]:
- 3 skeins

Scarf
- 375{425} yards [343{389} meters]

Hat
- 165{200} yards [151{183} meters]

- **Crochet Hook**

Child
- Size H (5 mm) **or** size needed for gauge

Adult
- Size I (5.5 mm) **or** size needed for gauge

- **Additional Supplies**
- Yarn needle

STITCH GUIDE

FRONT POST
DOUBLE CROCHET
(abbreviated FPdc)

YO, insert hook from **front** to **back** around post of st indicated one row/rnd **below** next st *(Fig. 6, page 156)*, YO and pull up a loop even with last st made (3 loops on hook), (YO and draw through 2 loops on hook) twice.

SINGLE CROCHET
2 TOGETHER
(abbreviated sc2tog)

Pull up a loop in each of next 2 sts, YO and draw through all 3 loops on hook **(counts as one sc)**.

SINGLE CROCHET
3 TOGETHER
(abbreviated sc3tog)

Pull up a loop in each of next 3 sts, YO and draw through all 4 loops on hook **(counts as one sc)**.

SCARF

Ch 25.

Row 1 (Right side)**:** Sc in second ch from hook and in each ch across: 24 sc.

Row 2: Ch 1, turn; sc in each sc across.

Row 3: Ch 1, turn; sc in first 2 sc, place marker around last sc made for st placement, sc in each sc across.

Row 4: Ch 1, turn; sc in each sc across.

Row 5: Ch 1, turn; sc in first 3 sc, work FPdc around marked sc on Row 3, skip next 3 sc on Row 3 from FPdc just made, work FPdc around next sc, ★ skip next 2 sc from last sc made, sc in next 3 sc, work FPdc around next sc on Row 3 from last FPdc made, skip next 3 sc on Row 3 from FPdc just made, work FPdc around next sc; repeat from ★ across to last 6 sc, skip next 2 sc from last sc made, sc in last 4 sc: 16 sc and 8 FPdc.

Row 6: Ch 1, turn; sc in each st across: 24 sc.

Row 7: Ch 1, turn; sc in first 2 sc, work FPdc around first 2-FPdc group one row **below**, skip next sc from last sc made, sc in next 3 sc, work FPdc around same 2-FPdc group as last FPdc made, ★ work FPdc around next 2-FPdc group one row **below**, skip next 2 sc from last sc made, sc in next 3 sc, work FPdc around same 2-FPdc group as last FPdc made; repeat from ★ across to last 3 sc, skip next sc from last sc made, sc in last 2 sc: 16 sc and 8 FPdc.

Row 8: Ch 1, turn; sc in each st across: 24 sc.

Row 9: Ch 1, turn; sc in first 4 sc, work FPdc around first FPdc one row **below**, ★ work FPdc around next 2-FPdc group one row **below**, skip next 2 sc from last sc made, sc in next 3 sc, work FPdc around same 2-FPdc group as last FPdc made; repeat from ★ 2 times **more**, work FPdc around last FPdc one row **below**, skip next 2 sc from last sc made, sc in last 3 sc: 16 sc and 8 FPdc.

Repeat Rows 6-9 for pattern until piece measures approximately 50¼{60}"/127.5{152.5} cm from beginning ch, ending by working Row 8.

Last Row: Ch 1, turn; sc in each sc across; finish off.

HAT

Ribbing
Ch 17.

Row 1 (Right side)**:** Sc in back ridge *(Fig. 2, page 155)* of second ch from hook and each ch across: 16 sc.

Rows 2-60: Ch 1, turn; sc in Back Loop Only *(Fig. 4, page 155)* of each sc across.

Joining Row: Ch 1, turn; hold beginning ch and last row with **right** side together, working in Back Loops Only of **each** layer, slip st in each st across; do **not** finish off.

Body

Rnd 1: Ch 1, sc in end of each row around; join with slip st to first sc: 60 sc.

Rnd 2: Ch 1; with **right** side facing, turn; sc in first 5 sc, 2 sc in next sc, (sc in next 5 sc, 2 sc in next sc) around; join with slip st to first sc: 70 sc.

Rnd 3: Ch 1, turn; sc in first 2 sc, place marker around last sc made for st placement, sc in each sc around; join with slip st to first sc.

Rnd 4: Ch 1, turn; sc in each sc around; join with slip st to first sc.

Rnd 5: Ch 1, turn; sc in first 3 sc, work FPdc around marked sc on Rnd 3, ★ skip next 3 sc on Rnd 3 from FPdc just made, work FPdc around next sc, skip next 2 sc from last sc made, sc in next 3 sc, work FPdc around next sc on Rnd 3 from last FPdc made; repeat from ★ around to last 2 sc, work FPdc around first sc (before first FPdc), skip last 2 sc from last sc made; join with slip st to first sc: 42 sc and 28 FPdc.

Rnd 6: Ch 1, turn; sc in each st around; join with slip st to first sc: 70 sc.

Rnd 7: Ch 1, turn; sc in first sc, work FPdc around last 2-FPdc group made one rnd **below**, ★ work FPdc around next 2-FPdc group one rnd **below**, skip next 2 sc from last sc made, sc in next 3 sc, work FPdc around same 2-FPdc group as FPdc just made; repeat from ★ around to last 4 sc, work FPdc around same 2-FPdc group as first FPdc (working it above first FPdc), skip next 2 sc from last sc made, sc in last 2 sc; join with slip st to first sc: 42 sc and 28 FPdc.

Rnd 8: Ch 1, turn; sc in each st around; join with slip st to first sc: 70 sc.

Rnd 9: Ch 1, turn; sc in first 3 sc, work FPdc around first 2-FPdc group made one rnd **below**, ★ work FPdc around next 2-FPdc group one rnd **below**, skip next 2 sc from last sc made, sc in next 3 sc, work FPdc around same 2-FPdc group as FPdc just made; repeat from ★ around to last 2 sc, work FPdc around same 2-FPdc group as first FPdc (working it above first FPdc), skip last 2 sc; join with slip st to first sc: 42 sc and 28 FPdc.

Rnd 10: Ch 1, turn; sc in each st around; join with slip st to first sc: 70 sc.

Rnds 11-22: Repeat Rnds 7-10, 3 times: 70 sc.

Shaping

Rnd 1: Ch 1, turn; work FPdc around last 2-FPdc group made one rnd **below**, work FPdc around next 2-FPdc group, skip first 3 sc, sc3tog, ★ work FPdc around same 2-FPdc group as FPdc just made, work FPdc around next 2-FPdc group one rnd **below**, skip next 2 sc from last sc made, sc3tog; repeat from ★ around to last 4 sc, work FPdc around same 2-FPdc group as FPdc just made, work FPdc around same 2-FPdc group as first FPdc (working it above first FPdc), sc3tog ending in first sc skipped; join with slip st to first FPdc: 14 sc and 28 FPdc.

Rnd 2: Ch 1, do **not** turn; beginning in same st as joining, (sc2tog, sc in next sc) around; join with slip st to first sc: 28 sc.

Rnds 3 and 4: Ch 1, beginning in same st as joining, sc2tog around; join with slip st to first sc: 7 sc.

Finish off leaving a long end for sewing.

Thread yarn needle with long end and weave it through sts on Rnd 4 *(Fig. 8, page 156)*; pull **tightly** to close and secure end.

Ring Time Necklace & Earrings Set

◐■▢▢ **EASY**

NED BY
ten
us Clay

Finished Measurements:

Necklace
Approximately 32" (81.5 cm) long
Earrings
Approximately (excluding ear wires)
2" (5 cm) long

Gauge Information:

Gauge Swatch:
Not crucial in this project;
use any size steel crochet
hook needed to achieve
desired look.

SHOPPING LIST

- **Thread** (Lace Weight) **⓪**
  [122 yards (111.5 meters) per ball]:
  - 20 yards (18.5 meters)

- **Steel Crochet Hook**
  - Size 7 (1.65 mm)

- **Additional Supplies**
  - Lever-back silver-tone ear wires - 2
  - 1" (2.5 cm) silver-tone hammered metal rings - 9
  - Chain-nose pliers - 2 pair

STITCH GUIDE

TREBLE CROCHET
(abbreviated tr)

YO twice, insert hook in st indicated, YO and pull up a loop (4 loops on hook), (YO and draw through 2 loops on hook) 3 times.

NECKLACE

First Side: Join thread with sc in first metal ring *(see Joining With Sc, page 154)*; 11 sc in same ring, ch 38, (12 sc in next metal ring, ch 38) 6 times; being careful **not** to twist, join with slip st to first sc, finish off: 7 ch-38 loops.

Second Side: Join thread with sc in opposite side of first ring; 11 sc in same ring, ch 15, 5 dc in next ch-38 loop, ch 15, ★ 12 sc in next ring, ch 15, 5 dc in next ch-38 loop, ch 15; repeat from ★ around; join with slip st to first sc, finish off.

EARRING *(Make 2)*

See Finishing Components, page 158.

Row 1: Join thread with sc in a metal ring; 11 sc in same ring: 12 sc.

Row 2: Ch 4, turn; tr in fourth ch from hook, ch 4, tr in fourth ch from hook, ch 6, skip first 4 chs from hook, slip st in next 2 chs (top loop made), (ch 4, tr in fourth ch from hook) twice, skip first 11 sc; join with slip st to last sc, finish off.

Using chain-nose pliers, open loop on ear wire. Insert loop into Earring top loop and close loop with pliers.

Fiesta Shawl

◖■☐☐ **EASY**

DESIGNED BY
Kristi Simpson

Finished Measurements:

14½" high x 55" wide (37 cm x 139.5 cm)
(before fringe)

....

SHOPPING LIST

- **Yarn** (Medium Weight) **4**
  [5.3 ounces, 518 yards
  (150 grams, 473 meters) per ball]:
  - 2 balls

- **Crochet Hook**
  - Size J (6 mm) **or** size needed
    for gauge

....

Gauge Information:

In pattern (Rows 1-6),
(2 dc, ch 2, 2 dc) 3 times = 5¼"
(13.25 cm); 6 rows = 4" (10 cm)

Gauge Swatch:

6"w x 4"h (15.25 cm x 10 cm)

Ch 21.

Work Body Rows 1-6, page 30:
14 dc and 3 ch-2 sps.

Finish off.

BODY

Ch 51.

Row 1 (Right side)**:** Working in back ridge of chs *(Fig. 2, page 155)*, sc in second ch from hook and in next ch, ★ ch 4, skip next 4 chs, sc in next 2 chs; repeat from ★ across: 18 sc and and 8 ch-4 sps.

Note: Loop a short piece of yarn around any stitch to mark Row 1 as **right** side.

Row 2: Ch 3 **(counts as first dc, now and throughout)**, turn; (2 dc, ch 2, 2 dc) in each ch-4 sp across, skip next sc, dc in last sc: 34 dc and 8 ch-2 sps.

Row 3: Ch 5 **(counts as first dc plus ch 2, now and throughout)**, turn; 2 sc in next ch-2 sp, (ch 4, 2 sc in next ch-2 sp) across to last 3 dc, ch 2, skip next 2 dc, dc in last dc: 18 sts and 9 sps.

Row 4: Ch 4 **(counts as first dc plus ch 1, now and throughout)**, turn; 2 dc in next ch-2 sp, (2 dc, ch 2, 2 dc) in each ch-4 sp across to last ch-2 sp, 2 dc in last ch-2 sp, ch 1, dc in last dc: 34 dc and 9 sps.

Row 5: Ch 1, turn; sc in first dc and in next ch-1 sp, ch 4, (2 sc in next ch-2 sp, ch 4) across to last ch-1 sp, sc in last ch-1 sp and in last dc: 18 sc and 8 ch-4 sps.

Row 6: Ch 3, turn; (2 dc, ch 2, 2 dc) in each ch-4 sp across, skip next sc, dc in last sc: 34 dc and 8 ch-2 sps.

Row 7: Ch 5, turn; 2 dc in next ch-2 sp, (ch 4, 2 dc in next ch-2 sp) across to last 3 dc, ch 2, skip next 2 dc, dc in last dc: 18 dc and 9 sps.

Row 8: Ch 4, turn; 2 dc in next ch-2 sp, (2 dc, ch 2, 2 dc) in each ch-4 sp across to last ch-2 sp, 2 dc in last ch-2 sp, ch 1, dc in last dc: 34 dc and 9 sps.

Row 9: Ch 1, turn; sc in first dc and in next ch-1 sp, ch 4, (2 sc in next ch-2 sp, ch 4) across to last ch-1 sp, sc in ch-1 sp and last dc: 18 sc and 8 ch-4 sps.

Row 10: Ch 3, turn; (2 dc, ch 2, 2 dc) in each ch-4 sp across, skip next sc, dc in last sc: 34 dc and 8 ch-2 sps.

Rows 11-19: Repeat Rows 3-10 once, then repeat Row 3 once **more:** 18 sts and 9 sps.

Row 20: Ch 3, turn; dc in next ch-2 sp, ch 4, (2 dc in next ch-4 sp, ch 4) across to last ch-2 sp, dc in last ch-2 sp and in last dc: 18 dc and 8 ch-4 sps.

Row 21: Ch 1, turn; sc in first dc, ch 2, 2 sc in next ch-4 sp, (ch 4, 2 sc in next ch-4 sp) across, ch 2, skip next dc, sc in last dc.

Rows 22-63: Repeat Rows 20 and 21, 21 times.

Rows 64-66: Repeat Rows 8-10.

Rows 67-86: Repeat Rows 3-10 twice, then repeat Rows 3-6 once **more.**

Finish off.

Holding 2 strands of yarn together, each 20" (51 cm) long, add fringe evenly across one long edge of Body *(Figs. 10a & b, page 157)*.

DESIGNED BY
Abbey Swanson

Classic Striped Socks

◖■▢▢▷ **EASY**

Finished Measurements:

Actual Foot Circumference:
Small - 7" (18 cm)
Medium - 8" (20.5 cm)
Large - 9" (23 cm)

Size Note: We have printed the instructions for the sizes in different colors to make it easier for you to find:

Small size = BLUE
Medium size = PINK
Large size = GREEN
All sizes = BLACK

··

SHOPPING LIST

- **Yarn** (Medium Weight)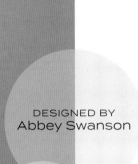
  [3 ounces, 197 yards
  (85 grams, 180 meters) per skein]:
  - MC (Cream) - 1 skein
  - CC (Grey) - 1 skein

- **Crochet Hook**
  - Size I (5.5 mm) **or** size needed
    for gauge

··

Gauge Information:

15 sc and 18 rnds = 4" (10 cm)

Gauge Swatch:
3½{4-4½}" wide flat x 1" high/
9{10-11.5} cm x 2.5 cm

Work same as Toe, page 34:
26{30-34} sc.

STITCH GUIDE

SINGLE CROCHET 3 TOGETHER
(abbreviated sc3tog)
Pull up a loop in each of next 3 sts, YO and draw through all 4 loops on hook **(counts as one sc)**.

TOE

With Contrasting Color, ch 8{10-12}.

Rnd 1 (Right side): Working in back ridge of chs *(Fig. 2, page 155)*, sc in second ch from hook and in each ch across to last ch, 3 sc in last ch; working in both remaining loops of beginning ch *(Fig. 3c, page 155)*, sc in same ch as last sc made and in next 6{8-10} chs, 2 sc in skipped ch; do **not** join, place marker to indicate beginning of rnd *(see Markers, page 154)*: 18{22-26} sc.

Rnd 2: ★ Sc in next 8{10-12} sc, 3 sc in next sc; repeat from ★ once **more**: 22{26-30} sc.

Rnd 3: Sc in next 9{11-13} sc, 3 sc in next sc, sc in next 10{12-14} sc, 3 sc in next sc, sc in next sc: 26{30-34} sc.

Rnd 4: Sc in each sc around.

Rnd 5: Sc in each sc around to last sc, sc in last sc changing to MC *(Fig. 5a, page 155)*; cut CC, remove marker.

FOOT

Sc in each sc around until piece measures 6{7-8}"/15{18-20.5} cm from beginning ch, or 2" (5 cm) less than desired length, ending at side with toe straight to re-establish sides of sock.

HEEL

Begin working in rows.

Row 1: Drop MC, with CC, ch 1, turn; sc in first 12{14-16} sc, leave remaining 14{16-18} sc unworked.

Rows 2-7: Ch 1, turn; sc in each sc across to last sc, leave last sc unworked: 6{8-10} sc.

Row 8: Ch 1, turn; 3 sc in first sc, sc in next 4{6-8} sc, 3 sc in last sc; sc in end of next row, slip st in unworked sc on next row: 11{13-15} sc.

Row 9: Turn; skip first slip st, sc in each sc across; sc in end of next row, slip st in unworked sc on next row: 12{14-16} sc.

Rows 10-13: Turn; skip first slip st, sc in each sc across; sc in end of next 2 rows, slip st in unworked sc on next row: 20{22-24} sc.

Row 14: Turn; skip first slip st, sc in each sc across to last sc, sc in last sc changing to MC, cut CC, place marker to indicate beginning of rnd.

LEG

Begin working in rnds.

Rnd 1: Do **not** turn; pull up a loop in end of last row on Heel and in first row and in same sc worked into on Foot, YO and draw through all 4 loops on hook, sc in next 14{16-18} sc on Foot, place second marker, pull up a loop in same st as first sc worked into on Heel and in end of next 2 rows, YO and draw through all 4 loops on hook, sc in each sc across to last sc, move rnd marker up: 36{40-44} sts.

Rnd 2: ★ Sc3tog, sc in each sc across to within one sc of next marker, move marker here; repeat from ★ once **more**: 32{36-40} sc.

Rnd 3: ★ Sc3tog, sc in each sc across to within one sc of next marker, remove marker; repeat from ★ once **more**: 28{32-36} sc.

Sc in each sc around until Leg measures 3½{4-4½}"/9{10-11.5} cm ending at back and changing to CC, do **not** cut MC; place marker to indicate beginning of rnd.

CUFF

Rnd 1: Sc in each sc around.

Rnd 2: Sc in each sc around changing colors in last sc; do **not** cut yarn.

Rnds 3-10: Repeat Rnds 1 and 2, 4 times.

Rnds 11-13: Sc in each sc around.

Rnd 14: Sc in each sc around changing colors in last sc; cut MC.

Rnds 15 and 16: Slip st in Back Loop Only of each st around *(Fig. 4, page 155)*.

Finish off.

Granny Square Shawl

DESIGNED BY
Michele Maks

▬▬◻◻◖ **EASY**

Finished Measurements:

Outer Edges - 49" (124.5 cm) long;
Inner Edges - 25" (63.5 cm) long

SHOPPING LIST

- **Yarn** (Medium Weight) 🔵**4**
  [3.5 ounces, 208 yards
  (100 grams, 190 meters) per skein]:
  - MC (Grey) - 4 skeins
  - Color A (Off White) - 1 skein
  - Color B (Dk Blue) - 1 skein
  - Color C (Gold) - 1 skein
  - Color D (Rose) - 1 skein

- **Crochet Hook**
  - Size J (6 mm) **or** size needed
    for gauge

Gauge Information:

Back = 23" (58.5 cm) square

Gauge Swatch:
6" (15.25 cm) square

Work same as Back, page 38,
through Rnd 4: 48 dc and
16 sps.

BACK

With Color C, ch 3; join with slip st to form a ring.

Rnd 1 (Right side): Ch 3 **(counts as first dc, now and throughout)**, 2 dc in ring, ch 3, (3 dc in ring, ch 3) 3 times; join with slip st to first dc: 12 dc and 4 ch-3 sps.

Note: Loop a short piece of yarn around any stitch to mark Rnd 1 as **right** side.

Rnd 2: Slip st in next 2 dc and in next ch-3 sp, ch 3, (2 dc, ch 3, 3 dc) in same sp, ch 1, ★ (3 dc, ch 3, 3 dc) in next ch-3 sp, ch 1; repeat from ★ 2 times **more**; join with slip st to first dc, finish off: 24 dc and 8 sps.

Rnd 3: With **right** side facing, join Color A with dc in any corner ch-3 sp *(see Joining With Dc, page 154)*; (2 dc, ch 3, 3 dc) in same sp, ch 1, 3 dc in next ch-1 sp, ch 1, ★ (3 dc, ch 3, 3 dc) in next corner ch-3 sp, ch 1, 3 dc in next ch-1 sp, ch 1; repeat from ★ 2 times **more**; join with slip st to first dc: 36 dc and 12 sps.

Rnd 4: Slip st in next 2 dc and in next corner ch-3 sp, ch 3, (2 dc, ch 3, 3 dc) in same sp, ch 1, (3 dc in next ch-1 sp, ch 1) twice, ★ (3 dc, ch 3, 3 dc) in next corner ch-3 sp, ch 1, (3 dc in next ch-1 sp, ch 1) twice; repeat from ★ 2 times **more**; join with slip st to first dc, finish off: 48 dc and 16 sps.

Rnd 5: With **right** side facing, join Color D with dc in any corner ch-3 sp; (2 dc, ch 3, 3 dc) in same sp, ch 1, ★ (3 dc in next ch-1 sp, ch 1) across to next corner ch-3 sp, (3 dc, ch 3, 3 dc) in corner sp, ch 1; repeat from ★ 2 times **more**, (3 dc in next ch-1 sp, ch 1) across; join with slip st to first dc: 60 dc and 20 sps.

Rnd 6: Slip st in next 2 dc and in next corner ch-3 sp, ch 3, (2 dc, ch 3, 3 dc) in same sp, ch 1, ★ (3 dc in next ch-1 sp, ch 1) across to next corner ch-3 sp, (3 dc, ch 3, 3 dc) in corner sp, ch 1; repeat from ★ 2 times **more**, (3 dc in next ch-1 sp, ch 1) across; join with slip st to first dc, finish off: 72 dc and 24 sps.

Rnds 7-18: Repeat Rnds 5 and 6, 6 times working in the following color sequence: 2 Rnds **each**, Color A, Color C, Color A, Color D, Color A, Color C: 216 dc and 72 sps.

FIRST EXTENSION

Row 1: With **right** side facing, join MC with dc in any corner ch-3 sp; 2 dc in same sp, ch 1, (3 dc in next ch-1 sp, ch 1) across to next corner ch-3 sp, 3 dc in corner sp, place a marker around same corner sp for Second Extension placement: 57 dc and 18 ch-1 sps.

Row 2: Ch 4 **(counts as first dc plus ch 1)**, turn; (3 dc in next ch-1 sp, ch 1) across to last 3 dc, skip next 2 dc, dc in last dc: 56 dc and 19 ch-1 sps.

Row 3: Ch 3, turn; 2 dc in next ch-1 sp, (ch 1, 3 dc in next ch-1 sp) across, leave last dc unworked: 57 dc and 18 ch-1 sps.

Rows 4-39: Repeat Rows 2 and 3, 18 times: 57 dc and 18 ch-1 sps.

Finish off.

SECOND EXTENSION

Row 1: With **right** side facing, join MC with dc in marked corner sp, do **not** remove marker; 2 dc in same sp, ch 1, (3 dc in next ch-1 sp, ch 1) across to next corner ch-3 sp, 3 dc in corner sp: 57 dc and 18 ch-1 sps.

Complete same as First Extension.

EDGING

Rnd 1: With **right** side facing, join Color B with sc in marked sp (between First & Second Extensions) *(see Joining With Sc, page 154)*, remove marker; † 2 sc in end of each row across Extension; working in sts and sps across last row of Extension, 3 sc in first st, sc in each st and in each sp across to last st, 3 sc in last st; 2 sc in end of each row across opposite side of Extension †; (sc in next sp and in next 3 dc) across to corner ch-3 sp on Back, 5 sc in corner sp, (sc in next 3 dc and in next sp) across to next Extension; repeat from † to † once; join with slip st to first sc: 620 sc.

Rnd 2: Ch 1, turn; sc in each sc around working 3 sc in center sc of each corner; join with slip st to first sc: 630 sc.

Rnd 3: Ch 2, do **not** turn; slip st in second ch from hook, skip next sc, ★ slip st in next sc, ch 2,

slip st in second ch from hook, skip next sc; repeat from ★ around; join with slip st at base of beginning ch-2, finish off.

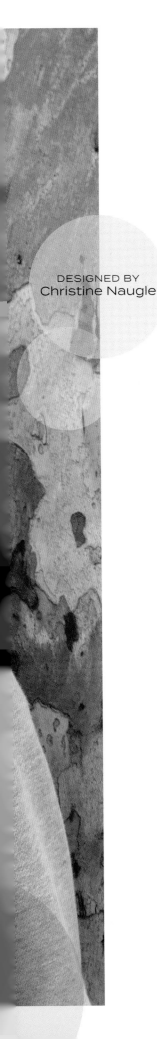

DESIGNED BY
Christine Naugle

Trail Creek Neck Warmer

 **EASY**

Finished Measurements:

5½" wide x 27" long (14 cm x 68.5 cm)

SHOPPING LIST

- **Yarn** (Medium Weight) **4**
  [5 ounces, 280 yards
  (140 grams, 256 meters) per skein]:
  - Variegated - 1 skein

  (Bulky Weight) **5**
  [3.5 ounces, 101 yards
  (100 grams, 92 meters) per skein]:
  - Off White - 1 skein

- **Crochet Hook**
  - Size I (5.5 mm) **or** size needed
    for gauge

- **Additional Supplies**
  - Yarn needle
  - ¾" (19 mm) Buttons - 2

Gauge Information:

In pattern,
13 sc and 16 rows = 4" (10 cm)

Gauge Swatch:
4" (10 cm) square

Row 1: With Variegated, work
13 fsc *(see Foundation Single
Crochet, page 154)*.

Rows 2-16: Ch 1, turn; sc in
each st across.

Finish off.

STITCH GUIDE

FRONT POST PUFF STITCH
(abbreviated FP Puff St)
(uses one st)

★ YO, insert hook from **front** to **back** around post of st indicated *(Fig. 6, page 156)*, YO and pull up a loop even with loop on hook; repeat from ★ once **more**, YO and draw through all 5 loops on hook.

FRONT POST SINGLE CROCHET
(abbreviated FPsc)
(uses one st)

Insert hook from **front** to **back** around post of st indicated *(Fig. 6, page 156)*, YO and pull up a loop, YO and draw through both loops on hook.

SINGLE CROCHET 2 TOGETHER
(abbreviated sc2tog)

Pull up a loop in each of next 2 sts, YO and draw through all 3 loops on hook **(counts as one sc)**.

NECK WARMER

Outer Section
The Outer section tends to curl as you crochet. This will be corrected as you crochet the Border.

Row 1 (Right side): With Variegated, work 17 fsc *(see Foundation Single Crochet, page 154)*.

Note: Loop a short piece of yarn around any stitch to mark Row 1 as **right** side.

Row 2: Ch 1, turn; sc in each st across.

Row 3: Ch 2 **(does not count as a st)**, turn; dc in first 2 sc, ch 1, skip next sc **(buttonhole made)**, dc in last 14 sc: 16 dc and one ch.

Row 4: Ch 1, turn; sc in each dc and ch across: 17 sc.

Row 5: Ch 1, turn; sc in first sc, (work FP Puff St around next sc, sc in next 3 sc) across.

Row 6: Ch 1, turn; sc in each st across.

Row 7: Ch 1, turn; sc in first 3 sc, work FP Puff St around first FP Puff St 2 rows **below**, skip next sc from last sc made, ★ sc in next 3 sc, work FP Puff St around next FP Puff St 2 rows **below**, skip next sc from last sc made; repeat from ★ once **more**, sc in last sc.

Row 8: Ch 1, turn; sc in each st across.

Row 9: Ch 1, turn; sc in first sc, work FP Puff St around next sc, sc in next 3 sc, ★ work FP Puff St around next FP Puff St 2 rows **below**, skip next sc from last sc made, sc in next 3 sc; repeat from ★ 2 times **more**.

Rows 10-99: Repeat Rows 6-9, 22 times; then repeat Rows 6 and 7 once **more**.

Rows 100-102: Ch 1, turn; sc in each st across.

BORDER
Rnd 1 (Right side): Turn; slip st in each sc across, ch 1; working in end of rows, sc in each sc row across working 2 sc in end of Row 3 (dc row), ch 1; slip st in ch at base of each fsc on Row 1, ch 1; working in end of rows, sc in each sc row across working 2 sc in end of Row 3 (dc row), ch 1; join with slip st to first slip st: 244 sts (206 sc, 34 slip sts, and 4 chs).

Rnd 2: Turn; slip st in first 4 sts, work FPsc around each of next 97 sc, slip st in next 4 sts; slip st in Front Loops Only of next 17 slip sts *(Fig. 4, page 155)*; slip st in **both** loops of next 4 sts, place a marker in last slip st made for Inner Lining placement, work FPsc around each of next 97 sc, slip st in next st, place a marker in st just made for Inner Lining placement, slip st in next 3 sts; slip st in Front Loops Only of last 17 slip sts; join with slip st to **both** loops of first slip st, finish off.

Inner Lining

Row 1: With **wrong** side facing, join Off White with slip st in first marked st, remove marker; (sc in next st, sc2tog) across ending in next marked st, remove marker: 65 sc.

Row 2 (Right side)**:** Ch 2, turn; dc in first sc, ★ ch 1, skip next sc, dc in next sc; repeat from ★ across: 33 dc and 32 ch-1 sps.

Note: Mark Row 2 as **right** side.

Rows 3-9: Ch 2, turn; skip first dc, dc in next ch-1 sp, ch 1, ★ skip next dc, dc in next ch-1 sp, ch 1; repeat from ★ across to last dc, dc in last dc.

Row 10 (Joining row)**:** Turn; with **wrong** sides of Inner Lining and Outer Section together, slip st in fourth st on opposite Border of Outer Section; ch 1, working through both layers, sc in first dc of Inner Lining **and** corresponding st of Border, ★ working in ch-1 sp of Inner Lining and next 2 sts of Border, sc2tog, sc in next dc of Inner Lining and next st of Border; repeat from ★ across; finish off.

Sew buttons to **right** side of Outer Section (on 2nd and 16th sts of Row 101).

Textured Stripes

DESIGNED BY
Lisa Gentry

 **EASY**

Finished Measurements:

Fits Head Circumference:
Small/Medium - 20½" (52 cm)
Large/X-Large - 22¼" (56 cm)

Size Note: We have printed the instructions for the sizes in different colors to make it easier for you to find:

Small/Medium size = PINK
Large/X-Large size = GREEN
All sizes = BLACK

Gauge Information:
Rnds 1-4 = 4¼" (10.75 cm);
14 sc = 4" (10 cm)

Gauge Swatch:
4¼" (10.75 cm) diameter

Work same as Hat, page 46, through Rnd 4; do **not** finish off: 48 dc.

SHOPPING LIST

▪ **Yarn** (Medium Weight) 🧶**4**
[3.5 ounces, 223 yards
(100 grams, 205 meters) per skein]:
 ▫ MC (Brown) - 1 skein
 ▫ CC (Grey) - 1 skein

▪ **Crochet Hook**
 ▫ Size H (5 mm) **or** size needed for gauge

STITCH GUIDE

FRONT POST DOUBLE CROCHET
(abbreviated FPdc)

YO, insert hook from **front** to **back** around post of st indicated *(Fig. 6, page 156)*, YO and pull up a loop even with loop on hook (3 loops on hook), (YO and draw through 2 loops on hook) twice.

HAT

With MC, ch 4; join with slip st to form a ring.

Rnd 1 (Right side)**:** Ch 3 **(counts as first dc, now and throughout)**, 11 dc in ring; join with slip st to first dc: 12 dc.

Rnd 2: Ch 3, dc in same st, 2 dc in next dc and in each dc around; join with slip st to first dc: 24 dc.

Rnd 3: Ch 3, 2 dc in next dc, (dc in next dc, 2 dc in next dc) around; join with slip st to first dc: 36 dc.

Rnd 4: Ch 3, dc in next dc, 2 dc in next dc, (dc in next 2 dc, 2 dc in next dc) around; join with slip st to first dc: 48 dc.

Rnd 5: Ch 3, dc in next 2 dc, 2 dc in next dc, (dc in next 3 dc, 2 dc in next dc) around; join with slip st to first dc: 60 dc.

Size Small/Medium ONLY
Rnd 6: Ch 3, dc in next 3 dc, 2 dc in next dc, (dc in next 4 dc, 2 dc in next dc) around; join with slip st to first dc: 72 dc.

Size Large/X-Large ONLY
Rnd 6: Ch 3, dc in next 3 dc, 2 dc in next dc, dc in next 4 dc, 3 dc in next dc, ★ dc in next 4 dc, 2 dc in next dc, dc in next 4 dc, 3 dc in next dc; repeat from ★ around; join with slip st to first dc: 78 dc.

Both Sizes
Rnds 7-10: Ch 3, dc in next dc and in each dc around; join with slip st to first dc.

Rnd 11: Ch 3, dc in next dc and in each dc around; join CC with slip st to first dc; do **not** cut MC.

Rnd 12: Ch 2 **(counts as first hdc, now and throughout)**, hdc in next dc, work FPdc around next dc, ★ hdc in next 2 dc, work FPdc around next dc; repeat from ★ around; join MC with slip st to first hdc; do **not** cut CC: 24{26} FPdc and 48{52} hdc.

Rnd 13: Ch 3, dc in next hdc, work FPdc around next FPdc, (dc in next 2 hdc, work FPdc around next FPdc) around; join with slip st to first dc.

Rnd 14: Ch 3, dc in next dc, work FPdc around next FPdc, (dc in next 2 dc, work FPdc around next FPdc) around; join CC with slip st to first dc; do **not** cut MC.

Rnd 15: Ch 2, hdc in next dc, work FPdc around next FPdc, (hdc in next 2 dc, work FPdc around next FPdc) around; join MC with slip st to first hdc; do **not** cut CC.

Rnds 16-25: Repeat Rnds 13-15, 3 times; then repeat Rnd 13 once **more**.

Cut CC.

Rnds 26 and 27 (Band)**:** Ch 1, sc in same st as joining and in each st around; join with slip st to first sc.

Finish off.

XOXO Tote

DESIGNED BY
Kristi Simpson

 **EASY**

Finished Measurements:

33¼" circumference x 10½" high x
5½" deep (84.5 cm x 26.5 cm x 14 cm)

SHOPPING LIST

- **Yarn** (Medium Weight) **4**
  [7 ounces, 370 yards
  (198 grams, 338 meters) per skein]:
  - Color A (Blue) - 2 skeins
  - Off White - 1 skein
  - Color B (Coral) - 1 skein

- **Crochet Hook**
  - Size J (6 mm) **or** size needed
    for gauge

- **Additional Supplies**
  - Yarn needle

Gauge Information:

In modified sc,
13 sts and 12 rows = 4" (10 cm)

With double strand of yarn,
10 hdc and 8 rows = 4" (10 cm)

Gauge Swatch:

4" (10 cm) square

Holding 2 strands of Blue
together, ch 11.

Work same as Base, page 50,
for 8 rows: 10 hdc.

Finish off.

STITCH GUIDE

MODIFIED SINGLE CROCHET
(abbreviated modified sc)

Insert hook in next st, YO and pull up a loop, with hook **over** the working yarn *(Fig. A)*, pull working yarn through both loops on hook.

Fig. A

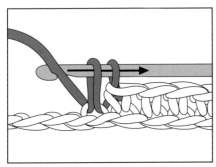

BASE

Holding 2 strands of Blue together, ch 44.

Row 1 (Right side)**:** Hdc in second ch from hook and in each ch across: 43 hdc.

Note: Loop a short piece of yarn around any stitch to mark Row 1 as **right** side.

Rows 2-11: Ch 1, turn; hdc in each hdc across; at end of Row 11, cut one strand of Blue.

BODY

Rnd 1: Using single strand of Blue, ch 1, sc in end of each row across; sc in free loops of each ch across *(Fig. 3b, page 155)*; sc in end of each row across; sc in each hdc across Row 11; join with slip st to first sc: 108 sc.

Begin working in Back Loops Only *(Fig. 4, page 155)* unless otherwise indicated.

Rnd 2: Ch 1, work modified sc in same st as joining and in each sc around; join with slip st to **both** loops of first modified sc.

Rnd 3: Ch 1, work modified sc in same st as joining and in each modified sc around; drop Blue, with Off White, join with slip st to **both** loops of first modified sc *(Fig. B)*.

Fig. B

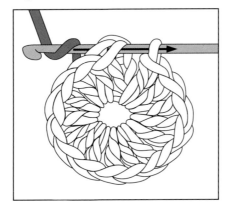

Rnd 4: Ch 1, work modified sc in same st as joining and in each st around; join with slip st to **both** loops of first modified sc changing to Blue; drop Off White.

Rnds 5 and 6: Repeat Rnds 3 and 4; at end of Rnd 6, cut Off White.

Rnd 7: Ch 1, work modified sc in same st as joining and in each st around; join with slip st to **both** loops of first modified sc changing to Coral; drop Blue.

Rnd 8: Ch 1, working over dropped color *(Fig. C)*, work modified sc in same st as joining and in next st changing to Blue in last st made *(Fig. D)*, drop Coral; ★ † work modified sc in next 3 sts changing to Coral in last st made, drop Blue; work modified sc in next 2 sts changing to Blue in last st made, drop Coral; work modified sc in next 4 sts changing to Coral in last st made, drop Blue; work modified sc in next 2 sts changing to Blue in last st made, drop Coral; work modified sc in next 3 sts changing to Coral in last st made, drop Blue †; work modified sc in next 4 sts changing to Blue in last st made, drop Coral; repeat from ★ 4 times **more**, then repeat from † to † once, work modified sc in last 2 sts; join with slip st to **both** loops of first modified sc.

Fig. C

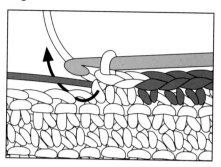

Fig. D

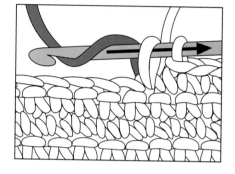

Rnds 9-15: Working in same manner, follow **Chart D**; at end of Rnd 15, join with slip st to **both** loops of first modified sc changing to Blue; cut Coral.

Rnds 16-19: Repeat Rnds 3-6.

Rnds 20-23: Ch 1, work modified sc in same st as joining and in each st around; join with slip st to **both** loops of first modified sc.

Rnd 24: Ch 1, work modified sc in same st as joining and in each st around; join with slip st to **both** loops of first modified sc changing to Off White; drop Blue.

Rnd 25: Ch 1, work modified sc in same st as joining and in each modified sc around; join with slip st to **both** loops of first modified sc changing to Blue; cut Off White.

Rnd 26: Ch 1, work modified sc in same st as joining and in each st around; join with slip st to **both** loops of first modified sc.

Rnd 27: Ch 1, work modified sc in same st as joining and in next 22 sts, ch 16, skip next 16 sts for first handle opening, work modified sc in next 38 sts, ch 16, skip next 16 sts for second handle opening, work modified sc in last 15 sts; join with slip st to **both** loops of first modified sc: 76 modified sc and 32 chs.

Rnd 28: Ch 1, work modified sc in same st as joining and in each st and each ch around; join with slip st to **both** loops of first modified sc: 108 modified sc.

Rnds 29-31: Repeat Rnds 24-26.

Finish off.

With yarn needle and a double strand of Coral, whipstitch around inside edge of each handle.

Chart D: TOTE

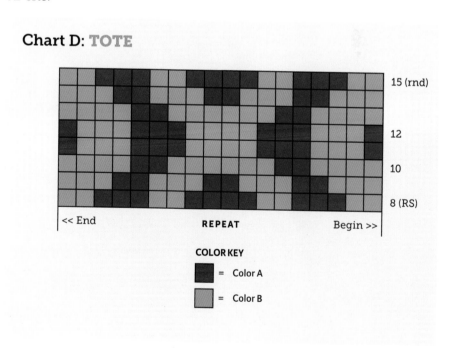

15 (rnd)

12

10

8 (RS)

<< End   REPEAT   Begin >>

COLOR KEY

■ = Color A

■ = Color B

On all rounds, follow **Chart D** from **right** to **left**.

Cables 'N Ribs

 **EASY**

DESIGNED BY
Melissa Leapman

Finished Measurements:

Headband: 21" circumference x 4" high (53.5 cm x 10 cm)

Hat: 21" (53.5 cm) circumference

Cowl: 68" circumference x 7" high (172.5 cm x 17.75 cm)

SHOPPING LIST

▪ **Yarn** (Bulky Weight) 🧶**5**
[3 ounces, 93 yards
(85 grams, 85 meters) per skein]:

Headband
⸽ 1 skein

Hat
⸽ 2 skeins

Cowl
⸽ 6 skeins

▪ **Crochet Hooks**

Headband and Hat
⸽ Size K (6.5 mm) **or** size needed
for gauge

Cowl
⸽ Size L (8 mm) **or** size needed
for gauge

▪ **Additional Supplies**
⸽ Yarn needle

Gauge Information:

Headband & Hat

With smaller size hook,
in pattern,
12 sts and 8 rows = 4" (10 cm)

Gauge Swatch:
4" (10 cm) square

Work same as Headband,
page 54, for 8 rows: 12 sts.

Cowl

With larger size hook, in
pattern, 9 sts = 3½" (9 cm);
6 rows = 5" (12.75 cm)

Gauge Swatch:
7" wide x 5" high
(17.75 cm x 12.75 cm)

Work same as Cowl, page 56,
for 6 rows: 18 sts.

STITCH GUIDE

FRONT POST DOUBLE CROCHET

(abbreviated FPdc)

YO, insert hook from **front** to **back** around post of st indicated *(Fig. 6, page 156)*, YO and pull up a loop even with last st made (3 loops on hook), (YO and draw through 2 loops on hook) twice.

BACK POST DOUBLE CROCHET

(abbreviated BPdc)

YO, insert hook from **back** to **front** around post of st indicated *(Fig. 6, page 156)*, YO and pull up a loop even with last st made (3 loops on hook), (YO and draw through 2 loops on hook) twice.

FRONT POST TREBLE CROCHET

(abbreviated FPtr)

YO twice, insert hook from **front** to **back** around post of st indicated *(Fig. 6, page 156)*, YO and pull up a loop even with last st made (4 loops on hook), (YO and draw through 2 loops on hook) 3 times.

FRONT POST DOUBLE TREBLE CROCHET

(abbreviated FPdtr)

YO 3 times, insert hook from **front** to **back** around post of st indicated *(Fig. 6, page 156)*, YO and pull up a loop even with last st made (5 loops on hook), (YO and draw through 2 loops on hook) 4 times.

HALF DOUBLE CROCHET 2 TOGETHER

(abbreviated hdc2tog)

(uses next 2 sts)

★ YO, insert hook in **next** st, YO and pull up a loop; repeat from ★ once **more**, YO and draw through all 5 loops on hook **(counts as one hdc)**.

FRONT POST DOUBLE CROCHET 2 TOGETHER

(abbreviated FPdc2tog)

(uses next 2 sts)

★ YO, insert hook from **front** to **back** around post of **next** st, YO and pull up a loop, YO and draw through 2 loops on hook; repeat from ★ once **more**, YO and draw through all 3 loops on hook.

HEADBAND

With smaller size hook, ch 13.

Row 1 (Right side): Hdc in third ch from hook **(2 skipped chs count as one hdc)** and in each ch across: 12 hdc.

Row 2: Ch 2 **(counts as first hdc, now and throughout unless otherwise specified)**, turn; hdc in next hdc and in each hdc across.

Row 3: Ch 2, turn; hdc in next hdc, skip next 3 sts, work FPdtr around each hdc one row **below** next 2 sts, hdc in third skipped st on Row 2, working in **front** of last 3 sts made, work FPdtr around each st one row **below** first 2 skipped sts, skip next 2 sts on Row 2, hdc in next st, work

FPtr around each st one row **below** next 2 sts, skip next 2 sts on Row 2, hdc in last 2 hdc.

Row 4: Ch 2, turn; hdc in next hdc and in each st across.

Row 5: Ch 2, turn; hdc in next hdc, work FPtr around each FPdtr 2 rows **below**, skip next 2 hdc on previous row, hdc in next hdc, skip next 2 FPdtr 2 rows **below**, work FPdtr around next 2 FPtr, skip next 2 hdc on previous row, hdc in next hdc, working **behind** previous 2 FPdtr, work FPdtr around each skipped FPdtr 2 rows **below**, skip next 2 hdc on previous row, hdc in last 2 hdc.

Row 6: Ch 2, turn; hdc in next hdc and in each st across.

Row 7: Ch 2, turn; hdc in next hdc, skip next 2 FPtr 2 rows **below**, work FPdtr around each of next 2 FPdtr, skip next 2 sts on previous row, hdc in next hdc, working in **front** of last 3 sts made, work FPdtr around each skipped FPtr 2 rows **below**, skip next 2 hdc on previous row, hdc in next hdc, work FPtr around each of next 2 FPdtr 2 rows **below**, skip next 2 hdc on previous row, hdc in last 2 hdc.

Repeat Rows 4-7 for pattern until piece measures approximately 21" (53.5 cm) from beginning ch when slightly stretched.

Finish off leaving a long end for sewing.

With wrong side together and using long end, sew seam matching sts of last row with free loops of beginning ch *(Fig. 3b, page 155)*.

HAT

Band
Work same as Headband, page 54.

Crown
Rnd 1: With **right** side of Band facing and using smaller size hook, join yarn with slip st at seam; ch 2, work 55 hdc evenly spaced around; join with slip st to first hdc: 56 hdc.

Rnd 2: Ch 2, hdc in next hdc and in each hdc around; join with slip st to first hdc.

Rnd 3: Ch 2, hdc in next hdc, work FPdc around each hdc one rnd **below** next 2 hdc (on Rnd 1), skip next 2 hdc on Rnd 2, ★ hdc in next 2 hdc, work FPdc around each hdc one rnd **below** next 2 hdc, skip next 2 hdc on Rnd 2; repeat from ★ around; join with slip st to first hdc: 28 FPdc and 28 hdc.

Rnd 4: Ch 2, hdc in next hdc, work FPdc around each of next 2 FPdc, ★ hdc in next 2 hdc, work FPdc around each of next 2 FPdc; repeat from ★ around; join with slip st to first hdc.

Repeat Rnd 4 for pattern until piece measures approximately 6" (15 cm) from bottom of Band.

Shaping

Rnd 1: Ch 2, hdc in next hdc, work FPdc around each of next 2 FPdc, ★ hdc2tog, work FPdc around each of next 2 FPdc; repeat from ★ around; skip beginning ch-2 and join with slip st to first hdc: 28 FPdc and 14 hdc.

Rnd 2: Ch 2, work FPdc around each of next 2 FPdc, ★ hdc in next hdc, work FPdc around each of next 2 FPdc; repeat from ★ around; join with slip st to first hdc.

Rnd 3: Slip st around post of next FPdc, ch 2, work FPdc around next FPdc, (skip next hdc, FPdc2tog) around; skip beginning ch-2 and join with slip st to first FPdc: 14 FPdc2tog.

Rnd 4: Ch 2, work FPdc around same FPdc, ★ YO, insert hook from **front** to **back** around post of first leg of next FPdc2tog, YO and pull up a loop, YO and draw through 2 loops on hook, YO, insert hook from **front** to **back** around post of second leg of same FPdc2tog, YO and pull up a loop, YO and draw through 2 loops on hook, YO and draw through all 3 loops on hook (one st made); repeat from ★ around; skip beginning ch-2 and join with slip st to first FPdc: 14 sts.

Rnd 5: Ch 2, work FPdc around same FPdc, FPdc2tog around; skip beginning ch-2 and join with slip st to first FPdc, finish off leaving a long end for sewing: 7 sts.

Weave yarn end through sts on Rnd 5 *(Fig. 8, page 156)*; pull **tightly** to close and secure end.

COWL

With larger size hook, ch 20.

Row 1: Dc in fourth ch from hook **(3 skipped chs count as first dc)** and in each ch across: 18 dc.

Row 2: Ch 2, turn; ★ work FPdc around each of next 2 sts, work BPdc around each of next 2 sts; repeat from ★ across to last st, hdc in last st.

Repeat Row 2 for pattern until piece measures approximately 68" (172.5 cm) from beginning ch.

Finish off leaving a long end for sewing.

Being careful **not** to twist piece and using long end, sew seam matching sts of last row with free loops of beginning ch *(Fig. 3b, page 155)*.

Make 10 tassels and attach evenly spaced along one long end of Cowl.

Tassel

Cut a piece of cardboard 4" (10 cm) wide and 7½" (19 cm) long. Wind the yarn lengthwise around the cardboard approximately 16 times. Cut an 18" (45.5 cm) length of yarn and insert it under all of the strands at the top of the cardboard; pull up tightly and tie securely. Leave the yarn ends long enough to attach the tassel. Cut the yarn at the opposite end of the cardboard and then remove it *(Fig. A)*. Cut a 10" (25.5 cm) length of yarn and wrap it tightly around the tassel twice, 1¼" (3 cm) below the top *(Fig. B)*; tie securely. Trim the ends.

Fig. A

Fig. B

Bead & Tassel Pendant

DESIGNED BY
Edie Eckman

◖■■☐☐◗ **EASY**

Finished Measurement:

Approximately 2½" (6.5 cm) diameter

SHOPPING LIST

- **Thread** (Lace Weight)
  [350 yards (320 meters) per ball]:
  - Purple - 1 ball
  - Olive - 1 ball
  - Orange - 1 ball

- **Steel Crochet Hook**
  - Size 2 (2.25 mm)

- **Additional Supplies**
  - 1" (25 mm) diameter decorative wooden bead (hole in bead must be large enough to accommodate 6 strands of thread)
  - 18" (45.5 cm) long Suede lace cord
  - Fold-over cord ends - 2
  - Craft glue
  - Lobster clasp
  - 10 mm Jump ring - 1
  - 6 mm Jump rings - 2
  - Tapestry needle
  - Chain-nose pliers (2 pair)

Gauge Information:

Gauge Swatch:
Not crucial in this project.

PENDANT

With Olive, ch 4; join with slip st to form a ring.

Rnd 1 (Right side): Ch 3 **(counts as first dc, now and throughout)**, 11 dc in ring; join with slip st to first dc, finish off: 12 dc.

Note: Loop a short piece of thread around any stitch to mark Rnd 1 as **right** side.

Rnd 2: With **right** side facing, join Purple with dc in any dc *(see Joining With Dc, page 154)*; 2 dc in same st as joining, (ch 1, skip next dc, 3 dc in next dc) 3 times, tie a short piece of thread around last dc made for hanging loop placement, ch 1, skip next dc, 3 dc in next dc, ch 1, skip next dc, dc in next dc, tie a short piece of thread around last dc made for hanging loop placement, 2 dc in same st, ch 1, skip last dc; join with slip st to first dc, finish off: 18 dc and 6 ch-1 sps.

Rnd 3: With **right** side facing, join Olive with dc in first dc of any 3-dc group; 2 dc in next dc, dc in next dc, 3 dc in next ch-1 sp, ★ dc in next dc, 2 dc in next dc, dc in next dc, 3 dc in next ch-1 sp; repeat from ★ around; join with slip st to first dc, finish off: 42 dc.

Rnd 4: With **right** side facing, join Orange with sc in any dc *(see Joining With Sc, page 154)*; (ch 1, skip next dc, sc in next dc) twice, ch 2, skip next dc, ★ sc in next dc, (ch 1, skip next dc, sc in next dc) twice, ch 2, skip next dc; repeat from ★ around; join with slip st to first sc, finish off: 21 sc and 21 sps.

Rnd 5: With **right** side facing, join Purple with dc in any sp; 2 dc in same sp, 3 dc in each sp around; join with slip st to first sc, do **not** finish off: 63 dc.

Rnd 6: Ch 1, working from **left** to **right**, work reverse sc in each dc around *(Figs. 9a-d, page 156)*; join with slip st to first sc, finish off.

Hanging Loop

With **wrong** side facing, join Purple with slip st around marked dc, remove marker; ch 6, slip st around next marked dc, remove marker; finish off.

Attach 10 mm jump ring around hanging loop.

Tassel

With **wrong** side facing and Hanging Loop at the top, tie a scrap piece of thread to center st at bottom edge for Tassel placement.

Cut one 12" (30.5 cm) strand **each** of Purple, Olive, and Orange. Hold the 3 strands together and thread strands through marked stitch. Align ends and tie an overhand knot close to the Pendant *(Fig. A)*. Thread these 6 strands through hole in the bead.

Fig. A

Cut two 10" (25.5 cm) strands **each** of Purple, Olive, and Orange. Holding these 6 strands together, tie them around the existing strands at the base of the bead, leaving equal

lengths on each side of knot. Tighten knot as much as possible. Smooth cut ends of tassel so that strands are parallel to each other.

Cut one 6" (15 cm) strand of Olive. Holding one end of the strand parallel to tassel, wrap remaining end **tightly** around the knot, securing cut end of strand and covering the knot. Secure end by running it through the knot several times. Cut end close to tassel. Trim tassel ends to 2¾" (7 cm) or to desired length.

Lay one suede end in one fold-over cord end, apply a drop of glue, and use the chain-nose pliers to fold the tabs down over the suede end *(Fig. B)*.

Repeat with the opposite end of the suede. Join one jump ring and lobster clasp to one fold-over cord end and the remaining jump ring to the other fold-over cord end. Thread cord through 10 mm jump ring.

Fig. B

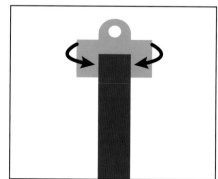

DESIGNED BY
Kristi Simpson

Color Splash

■■□□ EASY

Finished Measurements:

18" high x 47" wide (45.5 cm x 119.5 cm)
(before fringe)

SHOPPING LIST

- **Yarn** (Fine Weight) **2**
  [3.5 ounces, 317 yards
  (100 grams, 290 meters) per ball]:
  - Variegated - 2 balls
  - White - 2 balls
- **Crochet Hook**
  - Size J (6 mm) **or** size needed
    for gauge

Gauge Information:

In pattern,
12 sts = 4" (10 cm);
Rows 1-5 = 2¾" (7 cm)
Rows 1-20 = 11" (28 cm)

Gauge Swatch:

4" wide x 2¾" high
(10 cm x 7 cm)

With Variegated, ch 13.

Work Body Rows 1-5, page 64:
12 sc.

Finish off.

STITCH GUIDE

TREBLE CROCHET
(abbreviated tr)

YO twice, insert hook in st indicated, YO and pull up a loop (4 loops on hook), (YO and draw through 2 loops on hook) 3 times.

BEGINNING LINKED DOUBLE CROCHET
(abbreviated beginning linked dc)

Insert hook in second ch from hook, YO and pull up a loop, insert hook in first st of previous row, YO and pull up a loop (3 loops on hook), (YO and draw through 2 loops on hook) twice.

LINKED DOUBLE CROCHET
(abbreviated linked dc)

Insert hook in horizontal bar of previous linked dc *(Fig. A)*, YO and pull up a loop, insert hook in next st of previous row, YO and pull up a loop (3 loops on hook) *(Fig. B)*, (YO and draw through 2 loops on hook) twice *(Fig. C)*.

Fig. A

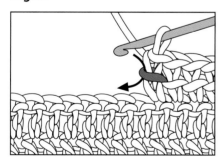

Fig. B

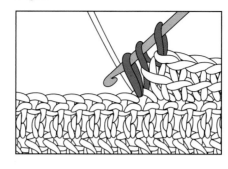

Fig. C

BODY

With Variegated, ch 55.

Row 1 (Right side): Sc in back ridge of second ch from hook and each ch across *(Fig. 2, page 155)*: 54 sc.

Note: Loop a short piece of yarn around any stitch to mark Row 1 as **right** side.

Row 2: Ch 2, turn; work beginning linked dc, work linked dc across.

Row 3: Ch 4 **(counts as first tr)**, turn; tr in next linked dc and in each linked dc across.

Row 4: Ch 2, turn; work beginning linked dc, work linked dc across.

Row 5: Ch 1, turn; sc in each linked dc across; finish off.

Row 6: With **wrong** side facing, join White with sc in first sc *(see Joining With Sc, page 154)*; ★ ch 3, skip next 3 sc, sc in next sc, skip next 2 sc, 3 dc in next sc; repeat from ★ across to last 4 sc, ch 3, skip next 3 sc, dc in last sc: 30 sts and 8 ch-3 sps.

Rows 7-20: Ch 1, turn; sc in first dc, ch 3, ★ sc in next dc, skip next 2 dc, 3 dc in next sc, ch 3; repeat from ★ across to last sc, dc in last sc; at end of Row 20, finish off.

Row 21: With **right** side facing, join Variegated with sc in first dc; 3 sc in next ch-3 sp, (sc in next 4 sts, 3 sc in next ch-3 sp) across to last sc, sc in last sc: 54 sc.

Rows 22-85: Repeat Rows 2-21, 3 times; then repeat Rows 2-5 once **more**.

Holding 3 strands of Variegated yarn together, each 10" (25.5 cm) long, add fringe evenly across one long edge of Body *(Figs. 10a & b, pages 156 & 157)*.

Everyday Set

▭▭▭▭▭ INTERMEDIATE

DESIGNED BY
Becky Stevens

Finished Measurements:

Scarf: 5{7}" wide x 45{57}" high [12.5{18} cm x 114.5{145} cm]

Hat: Fits 16½{19}"/42{48.5} cm head circumference

Size Note: We have printed the instructions for the sizes in different colors to make it easier for you to find:

Child size = BLUE
Adult size = PINK
All sizes = BLACK

....

SHOPPING LIST

- **Yarn** (Medium Weight) **4**
  [7 ounces, 364 yards (198 grams, 333 meters) per skein]:

  Complete Set
  - 2 skeins

  Scarf
  - 275 yards (251 meters)

  Hat
  - 145 yards (133 meters)

- **Crochet Hooks**

  Child
  - Size H (5 mm) **or** size needed for gauge

  Adult
  - Size I (5.5 mm) **or** size needed for gauge

- **Additional Supplies**
  - Yarn needle

....

Gauge Information:

Child: In pattern, (ex sc, ch 1) 7 times = 3¾" (9.5 cm); 7 rows = 2½" (6.25 cm)

Adult: In pattern, (ex sc, ch 1) 7 times = 4¼" (10.75 cm); 6 rows = 2¼" (5.75 cm)

Gauge Swatches

Child: 5¼"w x 4"h (13.25 cm x 10 cm)

Work same as Scarf, page 68, for 7 rows: 10 ex sc and 9 ch-1 sps.

Adult: 6"w x 3¼"h (15.25 cm x 8.25 cm)

Work same as Scarf, page 68, for 7 rows: 12 ex sc and 11 ch-1 sps.

STITCH GUIDE

EXTENDED SINGLE CROCHET
(abbreviated ex sc)

Insert hook in st or sp indicated, YO and pull a loop, YO and draw through one loop on hook, YO and draw through both loops on hook.

EXTENDED SINGLE CROCHET 2 TOGETHER
(abbreviated ex sc2tog)

★ Insert hook in **next** st, YO and pull up a loop, YO and draw through one loop on hook; repeat from ★ once **more**, YO and draw through all 3 loops on hook **(counts as one ex sc)**.

SCARF

Ch 20{24}.

Row 1 (Right side)**:** Ex sc in fourth ch from hook **(3 skipped chs count as first ex sc plus ch 1)**, ★ ch 1, skip next ch, ex sc in next ch; repeat from ★ across: 10{12} ex sc and 9{11} ch-1 sps.

Note: Loop a short piece of yarn around any stitch to mark Row 1 as **right** side.

Row 2: Ch 3 **(counts as first ex sc plus ch 1)**, turn; ex sc in first ch-1 sp, ★ ch 1, skip next ex sc, ex sc in next ch-1 sp; repeat from ★ across, leave last ex sc unworked.

Repeat Row 2 for pattern until Scarf measures approximately 44{56½}"/113{143.5} cm from beginning ch, ending by working a **wrong** side row; do **not** finish off.

Edging: Ch 1, turn; sc evenly around entire Scarf working 3 sc in each corner; join with slip st to first sc, finish off.

HAT

Ribbing
Ch 17.

Row 1 (Right side)**:** Sc in back ridge *(Fig. 2, page 155)* of second ch from hook and each ch across: 16 sc.

Rows 2-60: Ch 1, turn; sc in Back Loop Only *(Fig. 4, page 155)* of each sc across.

Joining Row: Ch 1, turn; hold beginning ch and last row with **right** side together, working in Back Loops Only of **each** layer, slip st in each st across; do **not** finish off.

Body
Rnd 1: Ch 1; with **right** side facing, sc in end of each row around; join with slip st to first sc: 60 sc.

Rnd 2: Ch 3 **(counts as first ex sc plus ch 1, now and throughout)**, do **not** turn; ex sc in next sc, ch 1, ★ skip next sc, ex sc in next sc, ch 1; repeat from ★ around; join with slip st to first ex sc: 31 ex sc and 31 ch-1 sps.

Rnds 3-12: Slip st in next ch-1 sp, ch 3, skip next ex sc, ★ ex sc in next ch-1 sp, ch 1, skip next ex sc; repeat from ★ around; join with slip st to first ex sc.

SHAPING
Rnd 1: Slip st in next ch-1 sp, ch 2 **(counts as first ex sc, now and throughout)**, ex sc in next ch-1 sp and in each ch-1 sp around; join with slip st to first ex sc: 31 ex sc.

Rnd 2: Ch 2, turn; ★ work ex sc2tog, ex sc in next ex sc; repeat from ★ around; join with slip st to first ex sc: 21 ex sc.

Rnds 3 and 4: Ch 2, turn; work ex sc2tog around; join with slip st to first ex sc: 6 ex sc.

Thread yarn needle with long end and weave it through sts on Rnd 4; *(Fig. 8, page 156)* pull **tightly** to close and secure end.

DESIGNED BY
Abbey Swanson

Trellised Rosebuds Socks

■■□□ **EASY**

Finished Measurements:

Actual Foot Circumference:
Small - 7" (18 cm)
Medium - 8" (20.5 cm)
Large - 9" (23 cm)

Size Note: We have printed the instructions for the sizes in different colors to make it easier for you to find:

Small size = BLUE
Medium size = PINK
Large size - GREEN
All sizes = BLACK

SHOPPING LIST

- **Yarn** (Medium Weight)
  [3.5 ounces, 200 yards
  (100 grams, 183 meters) per skein]:
  - 2 skeins

- **Crochet Hook**
  - Size I (5.5 mm) **or** size needed for gauge

Gauge Information:

15 sc and 18 rnds = 4" (10 cm)

Gauge Swatch:
3½{4-4½}" wide flat x 1" high/9{10-11.5} cm x 2.5 cm

Work same as Toe, page 72:
26{30-34} sc.

STITCH GUIDE

SINGLE CROCHET 3 TOGETHER
(abbreviated sc3tog)

Pull up a loop in each of next 3 sts, YO and draw through all 4 loops on hook (**counts as one sc**).

CLUSTER
(uses one ch-1 sp)

★ YO, insert hook in ch-1 sp indicated, YO and pull up a loop, YO and draw through 2 loops on hook; repeat from ★ 3 times **more**, YO and draw through all 5 loops on hook.

FRONT POST DOUBLE CROCHET
(abbreviated FPdc)

YO, insert hook from **front** to **back** around post of dc indicated *(Fig. 6, page 156)*, YO and pull up a loop (3 loops on hook), (YO and draw through 2 loops on hook) twice.

TOE

Ch 8{10-12}.

Rnd 1 (Right side): Working in back ridge of chs *(Fig. 2, page 155)*, sc in second ch from hook and in each ch across to last ch, 3 sc in last ch; working in both remaining loops of beginning ch *(Fig. 3c, page 155)*, sc in same ch as last sc made and in next 6{8-10} chs, 2 sc in skipped ch; do **not** join, place marker to indicate beginning of rnd *(see Markers, page 154)*: 18{22-26} sc.

Rnd 2: ★ Sc in next 8{10-12} sc, 3 sc in next sc; repeat from ★ once **more**: 22{26-30} sc.

Rnd 3: Sc in next 9{11-13} sc, 3 sc in next sc, sc in next 10{12-14} sc, 3 sc in next sc, sc in next sc; remove marker: 26{30-34} sc.

FOOT

Sc in each sc around until piece measures 6{7-8}"/15{18-20.5} cm from beginning ch, or 2" (5 cm) less than desired length, ending at side with toe straight to re-establish sides of sock.

HEEL

Begin working in rows.

Row 1: Ch 1, turn; sc in first 12{14-16} sc, leave remaining 14{16-18} sc unworked.

Rows 2-7: Ch 1, turn; sc in each sc across to last sc, leave remaining sc unworked: 6{8-10} sc.

Row 8: Ch 1, turn; 3 sc in first sc, sc in next 4{6-8} sc, 3 sc in last sc; sc in end of next row, slip st in unworked sc on next row: 11{13-15} sc.

Row 9: Turn; skip first slip st, sc in each sc across; sc in end of next row, slip st in unworked sc on next row: 12{14-16} sc.

Rows 10-13: Turn; skip first slip st, sc in each sc across; sc in end of next 2 rows, slip st in unworked sc on next row: 20{22-24} sc.

Row 14: Turn; skip first slip st, sc in each sc across to last sc, place marker to indicate beginning of rnd.

LEG

Begin working in rnds.

Rnd 1: Do **not** turn; pull up a loop in end of last row on Heel and in first row and in same sc worked into on Foot, YO and draw through all 4 loops on hook, sc in next 14{16-18} sc on Foot, place second marker, pull up a loop in same st as first sc worked into on Heel and in end of next 2 rows, YO and draw through all 4 loops on hook, sc in each sc across to last sc, move rnd marker here: 36{40-44} sts.

Rnd 2: ★ Sc3tog, sc in each sc across to within one sc of next marker, move marker here; repeat from ★ once **more**: 32{36-40} sc.

Rnd 3: ★ Sc3tog, sc in each sc across to within one sc of next marker; repeat from ★ once more, remove second marker: 28{32-36} sc.

Rnds 4 and 5: Sc in each sc around.

Rnd 6: Remove marker, ch 1, ★ dc in next sc, skip next sc, (dc, ch 1, dc) in next sc, skip next sc; repeat from ★ around; join with slip st to first dc: 7{8-9} ch-1 sps and 21{24-27} dc.

Rnd 7: Ch 1, work FPdc around same st as joining, ch 1, work Cluster in next ch-1 sp, ch 1, ★ work FPdc around next dc, ch 1, work Cluster in next ch-1 sp, ch 1; repeat from ★ around; join with slip st to first FPdc: 7{8-9} Clusters and 7{8-9} FPdc.

Rnd 8: Ch 1, work FPdc around same st as joining, (dc, ch 1, dc) in next Cluster, ★ work FPdc around next FPdc, (dc, ch 1, dc) in next Cluster; repeat from ★ around; join with slip st to first FPdc: 7{8-9} ch-1 sps and 7{8-9} FPdc.

Rnds 9-19: Repeat Rnds 7 and 8, 5 times; then repeat Rnd 7 once **more**.

Rnd 20: Ch 1, sc in each st and in each ch-1 sp around; join with slip st to first sc: 28{32-36} sc.

Rnd 21: Ch 1, sc in each sc around; join with slip st to first sc, finish off.

Summery Silk Shrug

DESIGNED BY
Abbey Swanson

⬤◼☐☐ **EASY**

Finished Measurement:

One size fits most

SHOPPING LIST

- **Yarn** (Light Weight) 🧶3 LIGHT
  [2.2 ounces, 102 yards
  (65 grams, 93 meters) per ball]:
  - Grey - 2 balls
  - Gold - 2 balls
  - Blue - 2 balls

- **Crochet Hook**
  - Size 7 (4.5 mm) **or** size needed
    for gauge

Gauge Information:

In pattern,
16 sts = 4" (10 cm);
12 rows = 4¾" (12 cm)

Gauge Swatch:

4½" wide x 4¾" high
(11.5 cm x 12 cm)

With Grey, ch 19.

Work same as Body, page 76,
for 12 rows: 18 dc.

Finish off.

BODY

With Grey, ch 109.

Row 1 (Right side): Sc in second ch from hook and in each ch across: 108 sc.

Note: Loop a short piece of yarn around any stitch to mark Row 1 as **right** side.

Row 2: Ch 3 (**counts as first dc, now and throughout**), turn; dc in next sc, ch 2, ★ skip next 2 sc, dc in next sc, ch 2; repeat from ★ across to last 4 sc, skip next 2 sc, dc in last 2 sc: 38 dc and 70 chs.

Row 3: Ch 1, turn; sc in each st across changing to Gold in last sc (*Fig. 5a, page 155*): 108 sc.

Row 4: Ch 3, turn; dc in next sc and in each sc across changing to Blue in last dc (*Fig. 5c, page 155*).

Row 5: Ch 1, turn; sc in each dc across.

Row 6: Ch 3, turn; dc in next sc, ch 2, ★ skip next 2 sc, dc in next sc, ch 2; repeat from ★ across to last 4 sc, skip next 2 sc, dc in last 2 sc: 38 dc and 70 chs.

Row 7: Ch 1, turn; sc in each st across changing to Gold in last dc: 108 sc.

Row 8: Ch 3, turn; dc in next sc and in each sc across changing to Grey in last dc.

Row 9: Ch 1, turn; sc in each dc across.

Row 10: Ch 3, turn; dc in next sc, ch 2, ★ skip next 2 sc, dc in next sc, ch 2; repeat from ★ across to last 4 sc, skip next 2 sc, dc in last 2 sc: 38 dc and 70 chs.

Row 11: Ch 1, turn; sc in each st across changing to Gold in last sc: 108 sc.

Rows 12-15: Repeat Rows 4-7 changing to Grey at end of last row.

Row 16: Ch 3, turn; dc in each sc across changing to Gold in last dc.

Row 17: Ch 1, turn; sc in each dc across.

Row 18: Ch 3, turn; dc in next sc, ch 2, ★ skip next 2 sc, dc in next sc, ch 2; repeat from ★ across to last 4 sc, skip next 2 sc, dc in last 2 sc: 38 dc and 70 chs.

Row 19: Ch 1, turn; sc in each st across changing to Grey in last sc: 108 sc.

Row 20: Ch 3, turn; dc in next sc and in each sc across changing to Blue in last dc.

Row 21: Ch 1, turn; sc in each dc across.

Row 22: Ch 3, turn; dc in next sc, ch 2, ★ skip next 2 sc, dc in next sc, ch 2; repeat from ★ across to last 4 sc, skip next 2 sc, dc in last 2 sc: 38 dc and 70 chs.

Row 23: Ch 1, turn; sc in each st across changing to Grey in last dc: 108 sc.

Rows 24-27: Repeat Rows 16-19 changing to Blue at end of last row.

Row 28: Ch 3, turn; dc in next sc and in each sc across changing to Grey in last dc.

Row 29: Ch 1, turn; sc in each dc across.

Row 30: Ch 3, turn; dc in next sc, ch 2, ★ skip next 2 sc, dc in next sc, ch 2; repeat from ★ across to last 4 sc, skip next 2 sc, dc in last 2 sc: 38 dc and 70 chs.

Row 31: Ch 1, turn; sc in each st across changing to Blue in last dc: 108 sc.

Row 32: Ch 3, turn; dc in next sc and in each sc across changing to Gold in last dc.

Row 33: Ch 1, turn; sc in each dc across.

Row 34: Ch 3, turn; dc in next sc, ch 2, ★ skip next 2 sc, dc in next sc, ch 2; repeat from ★ across to last 4 sc, skip next 2 sc, dc in last 2 sc: 38 dc and 70 chs.

Row 35: Ch 1, turn; sc in each st across changing to Blue in last dc: 108 sc.

Rows 36-39: Repeat Rows 28-31 changing to Gold at end of last row.

Rows 40-63: Repeat Rows 4-27; at end of last row, finish off.

First Side Trim: With **wrong** side facing and working in end of rows, join Blue with sc in first sc on Row 1 *(see Joining With Sc, page 154)*; work 99 sc evenly spaced across; finish off: 100 sc.

Second Side Trim: With **wrong** side facing and working in end of rows on opposite side of Body, join Blue with sc in first sc on Row 63; work 99 sc evenly spaced across changing to Grey in last sc; do **not** finish off: 100 sc.

Border: Ch 1, turn; sc in each sc across to last sc, 2 sc in last sc; sc in each sc across Row 63; 2 sc in first sc on First Side Trim, sc in each sc across; finish off.

ASSEMBLY

Fold Body in half, having **wrong** side together and matching first and last rows of Body.

Joining: Working through **both** layers across short end and through **inside** loops of Border sts, join Grey with slip st in first sc; slip st in next 9 sc; do **not** finish off.

Arm Opening - Rnd 1: Continuing around single layer of Border, sc in both loops of each sc around *(Fig. 4, page 155)*; join with slip st to first sc.

Rnd 2: Ch 1, sc in same st as joining and in each sc around; join with slip st to first sc, finish off.

Repeat Joining and Arm Opening across opposite short end.

Outer Border - Rnd 1: With **right** side facing and working in free loops of beginning ch *(Fig. 3b, page 155)*, join Grey with sc in first ch; sc in each ch across; sc in each sc across Border; join with slip st to first sc.

Rnd 2: Ch 1, sc in same st as joining and in each sc around; join with slip st to first sc; finish off.

Granny Square Sling Tote

DESIGNED BY
Kristi Simpson

◖◼◻◻ **EASY**

Finished Measurements:

16" wide x 17" high (40.5 cm x 43 cm)

SHOPPING LIST

- **Yarn** (Medium Weight) **4**
  [3 ounces, 145 yards
  (85 grams, 133 meters) per skein]:
  - 3 skeins

- **Crochet Hook**
  - Size J (6 mm) **or** size needed
    for gauge

- **Additional Supplies**
  - Yarn needle
  - Leather strap
  - 2" (5 cm) Button
  - Sewing needle and thread

Gauge Information:

One Granny Square = 16"
(40.75 cm)

Gauge Swatch:

4¼" (10.75 cm) square

Work same as Granny Square,
page 80, for 3 rnds: 36 dc and
4 corner ch-3 sps.

STITCH GUIDE

TREBLE CROCHET
(abbreviated tr)

YO twice, insert hook in st indicated, YO and pull up a loop (4 loops on hook), (YO and draw through 2 loops on hook) 3 times.

SINGLE CROCHET 2 TOGETHER
(abbreviated sc2tog)

Insert hook in corner sp of **same** square, YO and pull up a loop, skip joining and insert hook in corner sp on **next** square, YO and pull up a loop, YO and draw through all 3 loops on hook.

GRANNY SQUARE
(Make 3)

Ch 4; join with slip st to form a ring.

Rnd 1 (Right side): Ch 3 **(counts as first dc, now and throughout)**, 2 dc in ring, ch 3, (3 dc in ring, ch 3) 3 times; join with slip st to first dc: 12 dc and 4 ch-3 sps.

Note: Loop a short piece of yarn around any stitch to mark Rnd 1 as **right** side.

Rnd 2: Ch 3, turn; (2 dc, ch 3, 2 dc) in first ch-3 sp, (3 dc, ch 3, 3 dc) in each of next 3 ch-3 sps; join with slip st to first dc: 24 dc and 4 ch-3 sps.

Rnd 3: Ch 3, turn; 2 dc in sp **before** next dc *(Fig. 7, page 156)*, skip next 3 dc, (3 dc, ch 3, 3 dc) in next ch-3 sp, skip next 3 dc, ★ 3 dc in sp **before** next dc, skip next 3 dc, (3 dc, ch 3, 3 dc) in next ch-3 sp, skip next 3 dc; repeat from ★ 2 times **more**; join with slip st to first dc: 36 dc and 4 corner ch-3 sps.

Rnd 4: Ch 3, turn; 2 dc in sp **before** next dc, (3 dc, ch 3, 3 dc) in next corner ch-3 sp, skip next 3 dc, ★ (3 dc in sp **before** next dc, skip next 3 dc) twice, (3 dc, ch 3, 3 dc) in next corner ch-3 sp, skip next 3 dc; repeat from ★ 2 times **more**, 3 dc in sp **before** next dc, skip next 3 dc; join with slip st to first dc: 48 dc and 4 corner ch-3 sps.

Rnds 5-8: Ch 3, turn; 2 dc in sp **before** next dc, skip next 3 dc, ★ (3 dc in sp **before** next dc, skip next 3 dc) across to next corner ch-3 sp, (3 dc, ch 3, 3 dc) in corner sp, skip next 3 dc; repeat from ★ 3 times **more**, (3 dc in sp **before** next dc, skip next 3 dc) across; join with slip st to first dc: 96 dc and 4 corner ch-3 sps.

Rnd 9: Ch 3, turn; dc in next dc and in each dc around working (4 dc, ch 1, 4 dc) in each corner ch-3 sp; join with slip st to first dc, finish off: 128 dc and 4 corner chs.

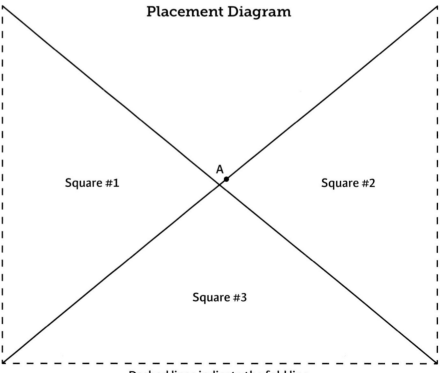

Placement Diagram

Square #1

A

Square #2

Square #3

Dashed lines indicate the fold line.

ASSEMBLY

Referring to **Placement Diagram**, page 80, fold each Granny Square in half and whipstitch Squares together working through **both** loops of each Square *(Fig. 4, page 155)*.

TRIM

With **right** side facing and referring to Point A on Placement Diagram, join yarn with sc in third dc before corner ch *(see Joining With Sc, page 154)*; sc in next 2 dc, sc2tog, sc in each dc across to within 2 dc of next corner ch, hold ring on strap parallel against **wrong** side edge of piece, working at the same time through sts or sp **and** ring, sc in next 2 dc, sc in next corner sp and in next 2 dc; working in dc on square ONLY, sc in each dc across to next corner ch, sc2tog, sc in each dc across to within 2 dc of next corner ch, hold ring on opposite end of strap parallel against **wrong** side edge of piece, working at the same time through sts or sp **and** ring, sc in next 2 dc, sc in next corner sp and in next 2 dc; working in dc on square ONLY, sc in each dc across; join with slip st to first sc, do **not** finish off.

Button Tab

Row 1: Ch 1, sc in same st as joining, dc in next 5 sc, sc in next sc, leaving remaining sc unworked: 7 sts.

Rows 2 and 3: Ch 3 **(does not count as a st)**, turn; dc in first st and in each st across.

Row 4: Ch 4 **(does not count as a st)**, turn; tr in first dc and in each dc across.

Row 5: Ch 3, turn; dc in first tr and in each tr across.

Row 6: Ch 1, turn; sc in each dc across; finish off.

Sew button on opposite side of Tote, buttoning between 2 tr on Tab.

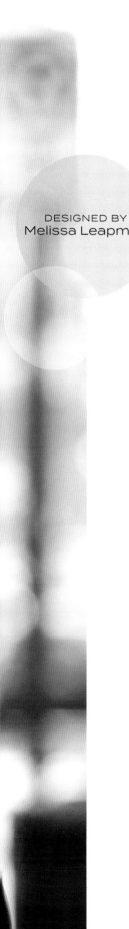

DESIGNED BY
Melissa Leapman

Modern Chullo

■■■◻ **INTERMEDIATE**

Finished Measurements:

Fits head circumference 20-22" (51-56 cm)

··

SHOPPING LIST

- **Yarn** (Medium Weight) **4**
  [3 ounces, 145 yards
  (85 grams, 133 meters) per skein]:
  - Dk Grey - 1 skein
    [3.5 ounces, 170 yards
    (100 grams, 156 meters) per skein]:
  - Color A (Red) - 1 skein
  - Color B (Grey) - 1 skein

- **Crochet Hook**
  - Size J (6 mm) **or** size needed for gauge

- **Additional Supplies**
  - Yarn needle

··

Gauge Information:

14 sc = 4" (10 cm);
5 rnds = 2¾" (7 cm)

Gauge Swatch:

2¾" (7 cm) diameter

Work same as Body, page 84,
for 5 rnds; do **not** finish off:
21 sc.

STITCH GUIDE

SINGLE CROCHET 2 TOGETHER
(abbreviated sc2tog)

Pull up a loop in each of first 2 sc, YO and draw through all 3 loops on hook **(counts as one sc)**.

CAP

Body

With Dk Grey, ch 4; join with slip st to form a ring.

Rnd 1 (Right side): Ch 1, 7 sc in ring; join with slip st to first sc.

Note: Loop a short piece of yarn around any stitch to mark Rnd 1 as **right** side.

Rnd 2: Ch 1, sc in same st as joining and in each sc around; join with slip st to first sc.

Rnd 3: Ch 1, 2 sc in same st as joining and in each sc around; join with slip st to first sc: 14 sc.

Rnd 4: Ch 1, sc in same st as joining and in each sc around; join with slip st to first sc.

Rnd 5: Ch 1, 2 sc in same st as joining, sc in next sc, (2 sc in next sc, sc in next sc) around; join with slip st to first sc: 21 sc.

Rnd 6: Ch 1, sc in same st as joining and in each sc around; join with slip st to first sc.

Rnd 7: Ch 1, 2 sc in same st as joining, sc in next 2 sc, (2 sc in next sc, sc in next 2 sc) around; join with slip st to first sc: 28 sc.

Rnd 8: Ch 1, sc in same st as joining and in each sc around; join with slip st to first sc.

Rnd 9: Ch 1, 2 sc in same st as joining, sc in next 3 sc, (2 sc in next sc, sc in next 3 sc) around; join with slip st to first sc: 35 sc.

Rnd 10: Ch 1, sc in same st as joining and in each sc around; join with slip st to first sc.

Rnd 11: Ch 1, 2 sc in same st as joining, sc in next 4 sc, (2 sc in next sc, sc in next 4 sc) around; join with slip st to first sc: 42 sc.

Rnd 12: Ch 1, sc in same st as joining and in each sc around; join with slip st to first sc.

Rnd 13: Ch 1, 2 sc in same st as joining, sc in next 5 sc, (2 sc in next sc, sc in next 5 sc) around; join with slip st to first sc: 49 sc.

Rnd 14: Ch 1, sc in same st as joining and in each sc around; join with slip st to first sc.

Rnd 15: Ch 1, 2 sc in same st as joining, sc in next 6 sc, (2 sc in next sc, sc in next 6 sc) around; join with slip st to first sc: 56 sc.

Rnd 16: Ch 1, sc in same st as joining and in each sc around; join with slip st to first sc.

Rnd 17: Ch 1, 2 sc in same st as joining, sc in next 7 sc, (2 sc in next sc, sc in next 7 sc) around; join with slip st to first sc: 63 sc.

Rnd 18: Ch 1, sc in same st as joining and in each sc around; join with slip st to first sc.

Rnd 19: Ch 1, 2 sc in same st as joining, sc in next 8 sc, (2 sc in next sc, sc in next 8 sc) around; join with slip st to first sc: 70 sc.

Rnd 20: Ch 1, sc in same st as joining and in next 33 sc, 2 sc in next sc, sc in next 34 sc, 2 sc in last sc; join with slip st to first sc changing to Grey *(Fig. 5d, page 155)*; cut Dk Grey: 72 sc.

When changing colors while working Rnds 23-29, carry unused color on **wrong** side of work with normal tension; do **not** cut yarn unless otherwise specified.

Rnds 21-31: Ch 1, sc in same st as joining and in each sc around following **Chart C**; join with slip st to first sc; at end of Rnd 29, cut Red and at end of Rnd 31, change to Dk Grey; cut Grey.

Rnds 32 and 33: Ch 1, sc in same st as joining and in each sc around; join with slip st to first sc.

Finish off.

Chart C: CAP

31 (rnd)
29
27
25
23
21 (RS)

End >> **REPEAT** << Begin

COLOR KEY

= Color A

= Color B

Always follow chart from **right** to **left**.

First Earflap

Row 1: With **right** side facing, skip first 11 sc and join Dk Grey with sc in next sc *(see Joining With Sc, page 154)*; sc in next 13 sc, leave remaining sc unworked: 14 sc.

Rows 2-11: Ch 1, turn; sc2tog, sc in next sc and in each sc across: 4 sc.

Row 12: Ch 1, turn; sc2tog, sc in last 2 sc: 3 sc.

Row 13: Ch 1, turn; sc2tog, sc in last sc: 2 sc.

Row 14: Ch 1, turn; sc2tog; finish off.

Second Earflap

Row 1: With **right** side facing, skip next 22 sc on Rnd 33 of Body from First Earflap and join Dk Grey with sc in next sc; sc in next 13 sc, leave remaining sc unworked: 14 sc.

Rows 2-11: Ch 1, turn; sc2tog, sc in next sc and in each sc across: 4 sc.

Row 12: Ch 1, turn; sc2tog, sc in last 2 sc: 3 sc.

Row 13: Ch 1, turn; sc2tog, sc in last sc: 2 sc.

Row 14: Ch 1, turn; sc2tog; finish off.

Trim

With **right** side facing, join Grey with sc in first sc on Rnd 33 of Body; sc in next 10 sc, † sc in same sc on Rnd 33 as first sc on Row 1 of Earflap; working in ends of rows on Earflap, skip first row, sc in next 12 rows, skip last row, 3 sc in sc on Row 14; skip first row, sc in next 12 rows, skip last row; sc in same sc on Rnd 33 as last sc on Row 1 of Earflap †, sc in next 22 sc on Rnd 33, repeat from † to † once, sc in last 11 sc; join with slip st to first sc, finish off.

Braid

Cut two 24" (61 cm) strands of each color yarn. Thread yarn needle with all 6 strands of yarn and pull yarn through center sc on one Earflap. With ends even, hold 4 strands of each color together. Work a 6½" (16.5 cm) braid; secure ends together with overhand knot, then trim ends.

Repeat for second Braid.

DESIGNED BY
Ruthie Marks

Scallops

 **EASY**

Finished Measurements:

6½" wide x 69" long (16.5 cm x 175.5 cm)

SHOPPING LIST

- **Yarn** (Medium Weight)
  [5 ounces, 251 yards
  (142 grams, 230 meters) per skein]:
  - Gold - 1 skein
  - Rust - 1 skein

- **Crochet Hook**
  - Size I (5.5 mm) **or** size needed
    for gauge

Gauge Information:

In pattern,
(dc, ch 1) 8 times = 4½"
(11.5 cm);
Rows 1-4 = 3¼" (8.25 cm)

Gauge Swatch:

6"w x 3¼"h
(15.25 cm x 8.25 cm)

With Gold, ch 24.

Work same as First Half,
page 89: 28 sts.

STITCH GUIDE

TREBLE CROCHET
(abbreviated tr)

YO twice, insert hook in sp indicated, YO and pull up a loop (4 loops on hook), (YO and draw through 2 loops on hook) 3 times.

CLUSTER

(uses one ch-1 sp)

★ YO, insert hook in ch-1 sp indicated, YO and pull up a loop, YO and draw through 2 loops on hook; repeat from ★ 2 times **more**, YO and draw through all 4 loops on hook.

FIRST HALF

With Gold, ch 248; place marker in fourth ch from hook for Second Half placement.

Row 1: Dc in sixth ch from hook **(5 skipped chs count as first dc plus ch 1 and one skipped ch)**, ★ ch 1, skip next ch, dc in next ch; repeat from ★ across: 123 dc and 122 ch-1 sps.

Row 2 (Right side): Ch 4 **(counts as first dc plus ch 1)**, turn; dc in next dc, (ch 1, dc in next dc) across.

Note: Loop a short piece of yarn around any stitch to mark Row 2 as **right** side.

Row 3: Ch 3 **(counts as first dc)**, turn; skip next 2 ch-1 sps, ★ work Cluster in next ch-1 sp, ch 6, work Cluster in next ch-1 sp, skip next 2 ch-2 sps; repeat from ★ across to last dc, dc in last dc: 60 Clusters, 2 dc, and 30 ch-6 sps.

Row 4: Ch 1, turn; sc in first dc and in next Cluster, ★ (hdc, 2 dc, 5 tr, 2 dc, hdc) in next ch-6 sp, sc in next 2 sts; repeat from ★ across; finish off.

SECOND HALF

Row 1: With **wrong** side facing and working in free loops of beginning ch *(Fig. 3b, page 155)*, join Rust with dc in first ch *(see Joining With Dc, page 154)*; ★ ch 1, skip next ch, dc in next ch; repeat from ★ across ending in marked ch, remove marker: 123 dc and 122 ch-1 sps.

Rows 2-4: Repeat Rows 2-4 of First Half.

Woven Bracelet

◼◼☐☐ **EASY**

DESIGNED BY
Edie Eckman

Finished Measurements:

1" wide x 7" circumference
(2.5 cm x 18 cm)

SHOPPING LIST

- **Thread** (Lace Weight) 🧵 **0** LACE
  [350 yards (320 meters) per ball]:
  - Purple -1 ball
  - Orange - 2½ yards (2.3 meters)
  - Aqua - 2½ yards (2.3 meters)
  - Yellow - 2½ yards (2.3 meters)
  - Pink - 2½ yards (2.3 meters)
- **Steel Crochet Hook**
  - Size 2 (2.25 mm)

Gauge Information:

23 sts = 3" (7.5 cm)

BAND

With Purple, ch 56; being careful **not** to twist ch, join with slip st to back ridge of first ch to form a ring *(Fig. 2, page 155)*.

Rnd 1 (Right side): Ch 4 **(counts as first dc plus ch 1, now and throughout)**, skip next ch, ★ dc in back ridge of next ch, ch 1, skip next ch; repeat from ★ around; join with slip st to first dc: 28 ch-1 sps.

Rnds 2-4: Ch 4, (dc in next dc, ch 1) around; join with slip st to first dc.

Finish off.

Cut six 14" (35.5 cm) strands of Orange. Holding strands together, weave through ch-1 sps of Rnd 1. Holding cut ends of strands together, tie ends in an overhand knot close to bracelet *(Fig. A)*; trim as desired.

Fig. A

Repeat with Aqua, Yellow, and Pink, weaving through sps of Rnds 2-4.

Gloves

 **EASY**

DESIGNED BY
Karen McKenna

Finished Measurements:

Finished Hand Circumference:
Child - 6½" (16.5 cm)
Medium Adult - 7½" (19 cm)
Large Adult - 8½" (21.5 cm)

Size Note: We have printed the instructions for the sizes in different colors to make it easier for you to find:

Child = BLUE
Medium Adult = PINK
Large Adult = GREEN
All sizes = BLACK

SHOPPING LIST

• **Yarn** (Light Weight) 3
[3.5 ounces, 340 yards
(100 grams, 310 meters) per skein]:
◦ One skein for all sizes

• **Crochet Hooks**
◦ Size G (4 mm) **or** size needed
for gauge

Additional Supplies
◦ Yarn needle

Gauge Information:

20 sc and 22 rows/rnds = 4"
(10 cm)

Gauge Swatch:
4" (10 cm) square

Ch 21.

Row 1: Sc in second ch from hook and each ch across:
20 sc.

Rows 2-22: Ch 1, turn; sc in each sc across.

Finish off.

STITCH GUIDE

SINGLE CROCHET 2 TOGETHER *(abbreviated sc2tog)*

Pull up a loop in each of next 2 sc, YO and draw through all 3 loops on hook **(counts as one sc)**.

FRONT POST DOUBLE CROCHET *(abbreviated FPdc)*

YO, insert hook **from** front to **back** around post of st indicated **(*Fig. 6, page 156)*,** YO and pull up a loop (3 loops on hook), (YO and draw through 2 loops on hook) twice.
Skip sc behind FPdc.

Start by choosing from three sizes and deciding whether to make regular gloves with or without touch screen slits, or fingerless gloves.

GLOVE

Cuff
Make one of the following Cuffs.

BASIC RIB
Ch 7{10-10}.

Row 1 (Wrong side): Sc in second ch from hook and in each ch across: 6{9-9} sc.

Note: Loop a short piece of yarn around the **back** of any stitch on Row 1 to mark **right** side.

Rows 2 thru 28{34-38}: Ch 1, turn; sc in Back Loop Only **(Fig. 4, page 155)** of each sc across.

Joining Row: Ch 1, turn; with **right** side together and matching last row and free loops of beginning ch **(Fig. 3b, page 154)**, slip st in each st across working through both thicknesses.

Continue with Body.

CABLED
Ch 8{10-10}.

Row 1 (Right side): Sc in second ch from hook and in each ch across: 7{9-9} sc.

Note: Loop a short piece of yarn around any stitch to mark Row 1 as **right** side.

Row 2: Ch 1, turn; sc in each sc across.

Row 3: Ch 1, turn; sc in first 2{3-3} sc, work FPdc around sc one row **below** each of next 3 sc, sc in last 2{3-3} sc: 4{6-6} sc and 3 FPdc.

Row 4: Ch 1, turn; sc in each st across: 7{9-9} sc.

Row 5: Ch 1, turn; sc in first 2{3-3} sc, skip next FPdc 2 rows **below**, work FPdc around next FPdc, work FPdc around skipped FPdc, work FPdc around next FPdc, sc in last 2{3-3} sc: 4{6-6} sc and 3 FPdc.

Row 6: Ch 1, turn; sc in each st across: 7{9-9} sc.

Row 7: Ch 1, turn; sc in first 2{3-3} sc, work FPdc around next FPdc 2 rows **below**, skip next FPdc, work FPdc around next FPdc, work FPdc around skipped FPdc, sc in last 2{3-3} sc: 4{6-6} sc and 3 FPdc.

Row 8: Ch 1, turn; sc in each st across: 7{9-9} sc.

Row 9: Ch 1, turn; sc in first 2{3-3} sc, work FPdc around each of next 3 FPdc 2 rows **below**, sc in last 2{3-3} sc: 4{6-6} sc and 3 FPdc.

Row 10: Ch 1, turn; sc in each st across: 7{9-9} sc.

Rows 11 thru 27{33-37}: Repeat Rows 5-10, 2{3-4} times; then repeat Rows 5 thru 9{9-7} once **more**: 4{6-6} sc and 3 FPdc.

Joining Row: Ch 1, turn; with **right** side together and matching last row and free loops of beginning ch **(Fig. 3b, page 154)**, slip st in each st across working through both thicknesses.

Continue with Body.

Body
Rnd 1 (Right side): Ch 1; with **right** side facing and working in end of rows, work 27{33-36} sc evenly spaced around; join with slip st to first sc.

Rnd 2: Ch 1, turn; sc in each sc around; join with slip st to first sc, do **not** finish off.

Medium Adult & Large Adult Sizes ONLY
Rnd 3: Ch 1, turn; sc in each sc around; join with slip st to first sc, do **not** finish off.

LEFT HAND - All Sizes
Rnd 3{4-4}: Ch 1, turn; sc in first 15{18-20} sc, 2 sc in each of next 2 sc, sc in last 10{13-14} sc; join with slip st to first sc: 29{35-38} sc.

Rnd 4{5-5}: Ch 1, turn; sc in first 11{14-15} sc, 2 sc in each of next 2 sc, sc in last 16{19-21} sc; join with slip st to first sc: 31{37-40} sc.

Rnd 5{6-6}: Ch 1, turn; sc in first 17{20-22} sc, 2 sc in each of next 2 sc, sc in last 12{15-16} sc; join with slip st to first sc: 33{39-42} sc.

Rnd 6{7-7}: Ch 1, turn; sc in first 13{16-17} sc, 2 sc in each of next 2 sc, sc in last 18{21-23} sc; join with slip st to first sc: 35{41-44} sc.

Rnd 7{8-8}: Ch 1, turn; sc in first 19{22-24} sc, 2 sc in each of next 2 sc, sc in last 14{17-18} sc; join with slip st to first sc: 37{43-46} sc.

Large Adult Size ONLY
Rnd 9: Ch 1, turn; sc in first 19 sc, 2 sc in each of next 2 sc, sc in last 25 sc; join with slip st to first sc: 48 sc.

Rnd 10: Ch 1, turn; sc in first 26 sc, 2 sc in each of next 2 sc, sc in last 20 sc; join with slip st to first sc: 50 sc.

All Sizes
Next 4{9-9} Rnds: Ch 1, turn; sc in each sc around; join with slip st to first sc.

Next Rnd: Ch 1, turn; sc in first 18{20-21} sc, ch 2{2-3}, skip next 7{8-11} sc (thumb opening), sc in last 12{15-18} sc; join with slip st to first sc: 30{35-39} sc and 2{2-3} chs.

Next 7{9-9} Rnds: Ch 1, turn; sc in each st around; join with slip st to first sc, at end of last rnd, do **not** finish off: 32{37-42} sc.

Continue with Digits - Both Hands.

RIGHT HAND - All Sizes
Rnd 3{4-4}: Ch 1, turn; sc in first 10{13-14} sc, 2 sc in each of next 2 sc, sc in last 15{18-20} sc; join with slip st to first sc: 29{35-38} sc.

Rnd 4{5-5}: Ch 1, turn; sc in first 16{19-21} sc, 2 sc in each of next 2 sc, sc in last 11{14-15} sc; join with slip st to first sc: 31{37-40} sc.

Rnd 5{6-6}: Ch 1, turn; sc in first 12{15-16} sc, 2 sc in each of next 2 sc, sc in last 17{20-22} sc; join with slip st to first sc: 33{39-42} sc.

Rnd 6{7-7}: Ch 1, turn; sc in first 18{21-23} sc, 2 sc in each of next 2 sc, sc in last 13{16-17} sc; join with slip st to first sc: 35{41-44} sc.

Rnd 7{8-8}: Ch 1, turn; sc in first 14{17-18} sc, 2 sc in each of next 2 sc, sc in last 19{22-24} sc; join with slip st to first sc: 37{43-46} sc.

Large Adult Size ONLY
Rnd 9: Ch 1, turn; sc in first 25 sc, 2 sc in each of next 2 sc, sc in last 19 sc; join with slip st to first sc: 48 sc.

Rnd 10: Ch 1, turn; sc in first 20 sc, 2 sc in each of next 2 sc, sc in last 26 sc; join with slip st to first sc: 50 sc.

All Sizes
Next 4{9-9} Rnds: Ch 1, turn; sc in each sc around; join with slip st to first sc.

Next Rnd: Ch 1, turn; sc in first 12{15-18} sc, ch 2{2-3}, skip next 7{8-11} sc (thumb opening), sc in last 18{20-21} sc; join with slip st to first sc: 30{35-39} sc and 2{2-3} chs.

Next 7{9-9} Rnds: Ch 1, turn; sc in each st around; join with slip st to first sc, do **not** finish off: 32{37-42} sc.

Continue with Digits - Both Hands.

DIGITS - BOTH HANDS
Pinkie
Rnd 1 (Wrong side)**:** Ch 1, turn; sc in first 4{5-5} sc, ch 2, skip next 25{28-31} sc, sc in last 3{4-6} sc; join with slip st to first sc: 7{9-11} sc and 2 chs.

Rnds 2 thru 4{5-6}: Ch 1, turn; sc in each st around; join with slip st to first sc: 9{11-13} sc.

Finish off for Fingerless Gloves ONLY.

Next 3{7-5} Rnds: Ch 1, turn; sc in each sc around; join with slip st to first sc.

Decrease Rnd: Ch 1, turn; sc in first sc, sc2tog 4{5-6} times; join with slip st to first sc, finish off leaving an 8" (20.5 cm) length for sewing: 5{6-7} sc.

Ring Finger

Rnd 1: With **wrong** side facing and having thumb opening to the left, join yarn with sc in first skipped sc after Pinkie *(see Joining With Sc, page 154)*; sc in next 3{3-4} sc, ch 2, skip next 17{19-21} sc, sc in next 4{5-5} sc, sc in free loops of next 2 chs on Pinkie; join with slip st to first sc: 10{11-12} sc and 2 chs.

Rnds 2 thru 5{6-8}: Ch 1, turn; sc in each st around; join with slip st to first sc: 12{13-14} sc.

Finish off for Fingerless Gloves ONLY.

Next 5{9-9} Rnds: Ch 1, turn; sc in each sc around; join with slip st to first sc.

Decrease Rnd: Ch 1, turn; sc in first 0{1-0} sc *(see Zeros, page 154)*, sc2tog 6{6-7} times; join with slip st to first sc, finish off leaving an 8" (20.5 cm) length for sewing: 6{7-7} sc.

Middle Finger

Rnd 1: With **wrong** side facing and having thumb opening to the left, join yarn with sc in first skipped sc after Ring Finger; sc in next 3{3-4} sc, ch 2, skip next 9{10-11} sc, sc in next 4{5-5} sc, sc in free loops of next 2 chs on Ring Finger; join with slip st to first sc: 10{11-12} sc and 2 chs.

Rnds 2 thru 6{6-9}: Ch 1, turn; sc in each st around; join with slip st to first sc: 12{13-14} sc.

Finish off for Fingerless Gloves ONLY.

Next 5{11-10} Rnds: Ch 1, turn; sc in each sc around; join with slip st to first sc.

Decrease Rnd: Ch 1, turn; sc in first 0{1-0} sc, sc2tog 6{6-7} times; join with slip st to first sc, finish off leaving an 8" (20.5 cm) length for sewing: 6{7-7} sc.

Index Finger

Rnd 1: With **wrong** side facing and having thumb opening to the left, join yarn with sc in first skipped sc after Middle Finger; sc in next 8{9-10} sc, sc in free loops of next 2 chs on Middle Finger; join with slip st to first sc: 11{12-13} sc.

Rnds 2 thru 5{6-6}: Ch 1, turn; sc in each sc around; join with slip st to first sc.

Finish off for Fingerless Gloves ONLY.

Next 5{9-11} Rnds: Ch 1, turn; sc in each sc around; join with slip st to first sc.

Decrease Rnd: Ch 1, turn; sc in first 1{0-1} sc, sc2tog 5{6-6} times; join with slip st to first sc, finish off leaving an 8" (20.5 cm) length for sewing: 6{6-7} sc.

Optional Touch Screen Slit For Adult Sizes ONLY

Rnd 1: With **wrong** side facing and having thumb opening to the left, join yarn with sc in first skipped sc after Middle Finger; sc in next {9-10} sc, sc in free loops of next 2 chs on Middle Finger; join with slip st to first sc: {12-13} sc.

Rnds 2 thru {10-12}: Ch 1, turn; sc in each sc around; join with slip st to first sc.

Left Hand - Rnd {11-13}: Ch 1, turn; sc in first 7 sc, ch {4-5}, skip next {4-5} sc, sc in last sc; join with slip st to first sc: 8 sc and {4-5} chs.

Right Hand - Rnd {11-13}: Ch 1, turn; sc in first sc, ch {4-5}, skip next {4-5} sc, sc in last 7 sc; join with slip st to first sc: 8 sc and {4-5} chs.

Next 4 Rnds: Ch 1, turn; sc in each st around; join with slip st to first sc: {12-13} sc.

Decrease Rnd: Ch 1, turn; sc in first {0-1} sc, sc2tog 6 times; join with slip st to first sc, finish off leaving an 8" (20.5 cm) length for sewing: {6-7} sc.

Thumb

Child Size ONLY - Rnd 1: With **wrong** side facing and having thumb opening to the left, join yarn with sc in first skipped sc; sc in next 6 sc, sc in free loops of next 2 chs; join with slip st to first sc: 9 sc.

Medium Adult Size ONLY - Rnd 1: With **wrong** side facing and having thumb opening to the left, join yarn with sc in same st worked into before first skipped sc; sc in next 8 skipped sc and in same st worked into after last skipped sc, sc in free loops of next 2 chs; join with slip st to first sc: 12 sc.

Large Adult Size ONLY - Rnd 1: With **wrong** side facing and having thumb opening to the left, join yarn with sc in same st worked into before first skipped sc; sc in next 11 skipped sc and in free loops of next 3 chs; join with slip st to first sc: 15 sc.

All Sizes
Rnds 2 thru 4{5-5}: Ch 1, turn; sc in each sc around; join with slip st to first sc.

Finish off for Fingerless Gloves ONLY.

Next 3{5-4} Rnds: Ch 1, turn; sc in each sc around; join with slip st to first sc.

Child Size ONLY -
Decrease Rnd: Ch 1, turn; sc in first sc, sc2tog 4 times; join with slip st to first sc, finish off leaving an 8" (20.5 cm) length for sewing: 5 sc.

Medium Adult Size ONLY -
Decrease Rnd: Ch 1, turn; beginning in first sc, sc2tog 6 times; join with slip st to first sc, finish off leaving an 8" (20.5 cm) length for sewing: 6 sc.

Large Adult Size ONLY -
Decrease Rnd: Ch 1, turn; sc in first sc, sc2tog 7 times; join with slip st to first sc: 8 sc.

Last Decrease Rnd: Ch 1, turn; beginning in first sc, sc2tog 4 times; join with slip st to first sc, finish off leaving an 8" (20.5 cm) length for sewing: 4 sc.

All Sizes
Thread yarn needle with end and weave needle through the sts on last Rnd *(Fig. 8, page 156)*; gather **tightly** to close and secure end.

Repeat at the end of each Digit.

Optional Touch Screen Slit For Adult Sizes ONLY
Medium Adult Size ONLY - Rnd 1: With **wrong** side facing and having thumb opening to the left, join yarn with sc in same st worked into **before** first skipped sc; sc in next 8 skipped sc and in same st worked into **after** last skipped sc, sc in free loops of next 2 chs; join with slip st to first sc: 12 sc.

Large Adult Size ONLY -
Rnd 1: With **wrong** side facing and having thumb opening to the left, join yarn with sc in same st worked into **before** first skipped sc; sc in next 11 skipped sc and in free loops of next 3 chs; join with slip st to first sc: 15 sc.

Both Sizes
Rnds 2 thru {4-6}: Ch 1, turn; sc in each sc around; join with slip st to first sc.

Left Hand - Rnd {5-7}: Ch 1, turn; sc in first {7-9} sc, ch {4-5}, skip next {4-5} sc, sc in last sc; join with slip st to first sc: {8-10} sc and {4-5} chs.

Right Hand - Rnd {5-7}: Ch 1, turn; sc in first sc, ch {4-5}, skip next {4-5} sc, sc in last {7-9} sc; join with slip st to first sc: {8-10} sc and {4-5} chs.

Next {5-2} Rnds: Ch 1, turn; sc in each st around; join with slip st to first sc: 15 sc.

Medium Adult Size ONLY -
Decrease Rnd: Ch 1, turn; beginning in first sc, sc2tog 6 times; join with slip st to first sc, finish off leaving an 8" (20.5 cm) length for sewing: 6 sc.

Large Adult Size ONLY -
Decrease Rnd: Ch 1, turn; sc in first sc, sc2tog 7 times; join with slip st to first sc: 8 sc.

Last Decrease Rnd: Ch 1, turn; beginning in first sc, sc2tog 4 times; join with slip st to first sc, finish off leaving an 8" (20.5 cm) length for sewing: 4 sc.

Both Sizes
Thread yarn needle with end and weave needle through the sts on last Rnd *(Fig. 8, page 156)*; gather **tightly** to close and secure end.

Repeat at the end of each Digit.

DESIGNED BY
Melissa Leapman

Brimmed Cap

 **EASY**

Finished Measurements:

Fits 20-22" (51-56 cm) head circumference

SHOPPING LIST

- **Yarn** (Medium Weight)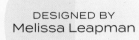
  [3 ounces, 145 yards
  (85 grams, 133 meters) per skein]:
  - 2 skeins

- **Crochet Hooks**
  - Size K (6.5 mm) **and**
  - Size L (8 mm) **or** sizes needed
    for gauge

- **Additional Supplies**
  - Straight pins
  - Yarn needle
  - Sewing needle
  - Matching thread
  - 1¼" (32 mm) Buttons - 2

Gauge Information:

Gauge Swatch:

4" (10 cm) diameter

Work same as Body, page 100,
for 4 rnds; do **not** finish off:
28 sc.

STITCH GUIDE

**BEGINNING SINGLE
CROCHET 2 TOGETHER**
(abbreviated beginning sc2tog)

Pull up a loop in each of first
2 sc, YO and draw through all
3 loops on hook **(counts as
one sc)**.

SINGLE CROCHET 2 TOGETHER
(abbreviated sc2tog)

Pull up a loop in each of next
2 sc, YO and draw through all
3 loops on hook **(counts as
one sc)**.

**Cap is worked holding two
strands of yarn together
throughout.**

CAP

Body

With larger size hook, ch 4; join with slip st to form a ring.

Rnd 1 (Right side)**:** Ch 1, 7 sc in ring; join with slip st to first sc.

Note: Loop a short piece of yarn around any stitch to mark Rnd 1 as **right** side.

Rnd 2: Ch 1, 2 sc in same st as joining and in each sc around; join with slip st to first sc: 14 sc.

Rnd 3: Ch 1, sc in same st as joining, 2 sc in next sc, (sc in next sc, 2 sc in next sc) around; join with slip st to first sc: 21 sc.

Rnd 4: Ch 1, sc in same st as joining and in next sc, 2 sc in next sc, (sc in next 2 sc, 2 sc in next sc) around; join with slip st to first sc: 28 sc.

Rnd 5: Ch 1, sc in same st as joining and in next 2 sc, 2 sc in next sc, (sc in next 3 sc, 2 sc in next sc) around; join with slip st to first sc: 35 sc.

Rnd 6: Ch 1, sc in same st as joining and in next 3 sc, 2 sc in next sc, (sc in next 4 sc, 2 sc in next sc) around; join with slip st to first sc: 42 sc.

Rnd 7: Ch 1, sc in same st as joining and in next 4 sc, 2 sc in next sc, (sc in next 5 sc, 2 sc in next sc) around; join with slip st to first sc: 49 sc.

Rnd 8: Ch 1, sc in same st as joining and in next 5 sc, 2 sc in next sc, (sc in next 6 sc, 2 sc in next sc) around; join with slip st to first sc: 56 sc.

Rnd 9: Ch 1, sc in same st as joining and in next 6 sc, 2 sc in next sc, (sc in next 7 sc, 2 sc in next sc) around; join with slip st to first sc: 63 sc.

Rnd 10: Ch 1, sc in same st as joining and in next 7 sc, 2 sc in next sc, (sc in next 8 sc, 2 sc in next sc) around; join with slip st to first sc: 70 sc.

Rnds 11 and 12: Ch 1, sc in same st as joining and in each sc around; join with slip st to first sc.

Rnd 13: Ch 1, sc in same st as joining and in next 7 sc, sc2tog, (sc in next 8 sc, sc2tog) around; join with slip st to first sc: 63 sc.

Rnd 14: Ch 1, sc in same st as joining and in next 6 sc, sc2tog, (sc in next 7 sc, sc2tog) around; join with slip st to first sc: 56 sc.

Rnd 15: Ch 1, sc in same st as joining and in next 5 sc, sc2tog, (sc in next 6 sc, sc2tog) around; join with slip st to first sc: 49 sc.

Rnd 16: Ch 1, sc in same st as joining and in next 4 sc, sc2tog, (sc in next 5 sc, sc2tog) around; join with slip st to first sc: 42 sc.

Rnd 17: Ch 1, sc in same st as joining and in next 11 sc, sc2tog, (sc in next 12 sc, sc2tog) twice; join with slip st to first sc: 39 sc.

Rnds 18-20: Ch 1, sc in same st as joining and in each sc around; join with slip st to first sc; at end of last rnd, do **not** finish off.

Brim

Change to smaller size hook.

Row 1 (Wrong side)**:** Ch 1, turn; sc in first 16 sc, leave remaining 23 sc unworked: 16 sc.

Rows 2-4: Ch 1, turn; work beginning sc2tog, sc in next sc and each sc across: 13 sc.

Row 5: Ch 1, turn; sc in Front Loop Only of each sc across **(Fig. 4, page 155)**.

Rows 6-8: Ch 1, turn; working in both loops, 2 sc in first sc, sc in next sc and each sc across: 16 sc.

Finish off, leaving a long end for sewing.

Thread yarn needle with long end. Fold Brim in half to **wrong** side and sew sc on Row 8 to sc on Rnd 20 of Body.

Trim: With **right** side facing, using smaller size hook, and working in end of rows through **both** layers of Brim, join yarn with sc in first row **(see Joining With Sc, page 154)**; sc in next 2 rows, 3 sc in corner, sc in free loops of each sc across Row 4 **(Fig. 3a, page 155)**, 3 sc in corner; sc in next 3 rows; finish off.

Strap

With smaller size hook, ch 23.

Row 1 (Right side): Sc in second ch from hook and in each ch across: 22 sc.

Note: Mark Row 1 as **right** side.

Row 2 (Buttonhole row): Ch 1, turn; sc in first sc, [ch 2, skip next 2 sc **(buttonhole made)]**, sc in next 16 sc, [ch 2, skip next 2 sc **(buttonhole made)]**, sc in last sc: 18 sc and 2 buttonholes (ch-2 sps).

Row 3: Ch 1, turn; sc in first sc, 2 sc in next ch-2 sp, sc in next sc and in each sc across to next ch-2 sp, 2 sc in next ch-2 sp, sc in last sc; finish off.

Finishing

Using photo as a guide for placement, pin the Strap above the Brim; sew buttons to Body behind the buttonholes.

Button Strap to the Cap.

DESIGNED BY
Abbey Swanson

Azure Dream

 **EASY**

Finished Sizes:

Small{Medium-Large}

Size Note: We have printed the instructions for the sizes in different colors to make it easier for you to find:

Small = BLUE
Medium = PINK
Large = GREEN
All sizes = BLACK

SHOPPING LIST

- **Yarn** (Light Weight) **3**
  [3.5 ounces, 245 yards
  (100 grams, 224 meters) per skein]:
  - Ecru - 1{2-2} skein(s)
  - Blue - 1{1-2} skein(s)

- **Crochet Hook**
  - Size 7 (4.5 mm) **or** size needed
    for gauge

Gauge Information:

17 dc = 4" (10 cm);
10 rows = 4¼" (10.75 cm)

Gauge Swatch:
4" wide x 4¼" high
(10 cm x 10.75 cm)

With Ecru, ch 19.

Row 1: Dc in fourth ch from hook **(3 skipped chs count as first dc)** and in each ch across: 17 dc.

Rows 2–10: Ch 3 **(counts as first dc)**, turn; dc in next dc and in each dc across.

Finish off.

STITCH GUIDE

TREBLE CROCHET
(abbreviated tr)

YO twice, insert hook in st or sp indicated, YO and pull up a loop (4 loops on hook), (YO and draw through 2 loops on hook) 3 times.

SINGLE CROCHET 2 TOGETHER
(abbreviated sc2tog)

Pull up a loop in each of next 2 dc, YO and draw through all 3 loops on hook **(counts as one sc)**.

DOUBLE CROCHET 2 TOGETHER
(abbreviated dc2tog)

(uses next 2 sts)

★ YO, insert hook in **next** st, YO and pull up a loop, YO and draw through 2 loops on hook; repeat from ★ once **more**, YO and draw through all 3 loops on hook **(counts as one dc)**.

DOUBLE DECREASE

(uses next 3 sts)

YO, † insert hook in **next** st, YO and pull up a loop, YO and draw through 2 loops on hook †, YO, skip **next** st, repeat from † to † once, YO and draw through all 3 loops on hook **(counts as one dc)**.

SHRUG

With Ecru and beginning at neck edge, ch 124; place marker in third ch from hook for Neck Trim placement.

Row 1 (Right side): Dc in fourth ch from hook **(3 skipped chs count as first dc)** and in next

23 chs, (dc, ch 1, dc) in next ch, dc in next 6 chs, (dc, ch 1, dc) in next ch, dc in next 56 chs, (dc, ch 1, dc) in next ch, dc in next 6 chs, (dc, ch 1, dc) in next ch, dc in last 25 chs: 126 dc, and 4 ch-1 sps.

Note: Loop a short piece of yarn around any stitch to mark Row 1 as **right** side.

Row 2: Ch 3 **(counts as first dc, now and throughout)**, turn; ★ dc in next dc and in each dc across to next ch-1 sp, (dc, ch 1, dc) in ch-1 sp; repeat from ★ 3 times **more**, dc in next dc and in each dc across: 134 dc and 4 ch-1 sps.

Rows 3 thru 11{12-13}: Ch 3, turn; ★ dc in next dc and in each dc across to next ch-1 sp, (dc, ch 1, dc) in ch-1 sp; repeat from ★ 3 times **more**, dc in next dc and in each dc across: 206{214-222} dc and 4 ch-1 sps.

Row 12{13-14}: Ch 3, turn; ★ dc in next dc and in each dc across to next ch-1 sp, ch 10{11-12}, skip ch-1 sp, next 28{30-32} dc, and next ch-1 sp (for armhole opening); repeat from ★ once **more**, dc in next dc and in each dc across: 150{154-158} dc and 20{22-24} chs.

Row 13{14-15}: Ch 3, turn; dc in next dc and in each dc and each ch across: 170{176-182} dc.

Row 14{15-16}: Ch 3, turn; dc in next dc and in each dc across to last dc increasing 1{0-0} dc **(see Zeros, page 154)**, dc in last dc changing to Blue

(Fig. 5c, page 155); cut Ecru: 171{176-182} dc.

Bottom Trim
Row 1: Ch 6 **(counts as first dc plus ch 3, now and throughout)**, turn; ★ skip next 4 dc, (dc, ch 2, dc) in next dc, ch 3; repeat from ★ across to last 5{5-6} dc, skip next 4{4-5} dc, dc in last dc: 68{70-72} dc and 67{69-71} sps.

Row 2: Ch 4 **(counts as first tr, now and throughout)**, turn; skip next ch-3 sp, (5 tr in next ch-2 sp, skip next ch-3 sp) across to last dc, tr in last dc: 167{172-177} tr.

Row 3: Ch 6, turn; skip next 2 tr, (dc, ch 2, dc) in next tr, ch 3, ★ skip next 4 tr, (dc, ch 2, dc) in next tr, ch 3; repeat from ★ across to last 3 tr, skip next 2 tr, dc in last tr: 68{70-72} dc and 67{69-71} sps.

Row 4: Ch 4, turn; skip next ch-3 sp, (5 tr in next ch-2 sp, skip next ch-3 sp) across to last dc, tr in last dc; finish off: 167{172-177} tr.

Neck Trim
Row 1: With **wrong** side facing and working in free loops of beginning ch **(Fig. 3b, page 155)**, join Blue with dc in marked ch **(see Joining With Dc, page 154)**, remove marker; dc2tog, dc in next 21 chs, double decrease, dc in next 4 chs, double decrease, dc in next 54 chs, double decrease, dc in next 4 chs, double decrease, dc in next 21 chs, dc2tog, dc in last ch: 112 dc.

Row 2: Ch 3, turn; dc2tog, dc in next 19 dc, double decrease, dc in next 2 dc, double decrease, dc in next 52 dc, double decrease, dc in next 2 dc, double decrease, dc in next 19 dc, dc2tog, dc in last dc; finish off: 102 dc.

Edging

With **right** side facing and working in tr on Row 4 of Bottom Trim, join Blue with sc in first tr *(see Joining With Sc, page 154)*; sc in same st and in next 2 tr, 3 sc in next tr, (sc in next 4 tr, 3 sc in next tr) across to last 3 tr, sc in next 2 tr, 3 sc in last tr; working in end of rows, 3 sc in first row, 2 sc in next row, 3 sc in next row, 2 sc in each of next 9{10-11} rows, † sc in next row, ch 31, slip st in second ch from hook and in each ch across (tie), sc in end of same row as last sc †, 2 sc in each of next 7 rows; working in dc across Row 2 of Neck Trim, 3 sc in first dc, sc in next 20 dc, sc2tog twice, sc in next 52 dc, sc2tog twice, sc in next 20 dc, 3 sc in last dc; working in end of rows, 2 sc in each of first 7 rows, repeat from † to † once, 2 sc in each of next 9{10-11} rows, 3 sc in next row, 2 sc in next row, 3 sc in next row, sc in same tr as first sc; join with slip st to first sc, finish off.

Armhole Edging

With **right** side facing and working in free loops of chs at underarm, join Blue with sc in first ch; sc in each ch across, 2 sc in side of next dc, sc in next ch-1 sp, sc in each unworked dc across to next ch-1 sp, sc in ch-1 sp, 2 sc in side of next dc; join with slip st to first sc, finish off.

Repeat around second armhole.

DESIGNED BY
Bonnie Barker

Cabled Backpack

■■□□ **EASY**

Finished Measurements:

14½" wide x 16½" long (37 cm x 42 cm)

SHOPPING LIST

- **Yarn** (Medium Weight) **4**
  [5 ounces, 245 yards
  (140 grams, 224 meters) per skein]:
  - 3 skeins (self-striping)

- **Crochet Hooks**
  - Size I (5.5 mm) **or** size needed
    for gauge
  - Size K (6.5 mm) (for Straps only)

- **Additional Supplies**
  - Macrame cord, ⅛" (3 mm)
    [50 yards (45.5 meters) per ball]:
  - 1 ball
  - Large wooden beads - 16
  - ¾ yard (.75 meter) fabric and matching
    thread for optional lining

Gauge Information:

In pattern,
16 sts (2 repeats) = 4½" (11.5 cm);
Rnds 1-6 = 3" (7.5 cm)

Gauge Swatch:

5¾" wide x 3" high
(14.5 cm x 7.5 cm)

Ch 22.

Row 1 (Right side): Dc in third
ch from hook **(2 skipped chs
count as first dc)** and in each
ch across: 20 dc.

Row 2: Ch 2 **(does not count
as a st, now and throughout),**
turn; work BPdc around first
st and each st across.

Row 3: Ch 2, turn; work FPdc
around each of first 2 BPdc,
★ skip next 2 sts, work FPtr
around each of next 2 sts,
working **behind** 2 FPtr just
made, work FPtr around each
of 2 skipped sts, skip next
2 sts, work FPtr around each
of next 2 sts, working in **front**
of 2 FPtr just made, work FPtr
around each of 2 skipped sts;
repeat from ★ once **more**,
work FPdc around each of last
2 BPdc.

Row 4: Ch 2, turn; work BPdc around first st and each st across.

Row 5: Ch 2, turn; work FPdc around each of first 2 BPdc, ★ skip next 2 sts, work FPtr around each of next 2 sts, working in **front** of 2 FPtr just made, work FPtr around each of 2 skipped sts, skip next 2 sts, work FPtr around each of next 2 sts, working **behind** 2 FPtr just made, work FPtr around each of 2 skipped sts; repeat from ★ once **more**, work FPdc around each of last 2 BPdc.

Row 6: Ch 2, turn; work BPdc around first st and each st across.

Finish off.

STITCH GUIDE

BACK POST DOUBLE CROCHET

(abbreviated BPdc)

YO, insert hook from **back** to **front** around post of st indicated *(Fig. 6, page 156)*, YO and pull up a loop (3 loops on hook), (YO and draw through 2 loops on hook) twice.

FRONT POST DOUBLE CROCHET

(abbreviated FPdc)

YO, insert hook from **front** to **back** around post of st indicated *(Fig. 6, page 156)*, YO and pull up a loop (3 loops on hook), (YO and draw through 2 loops on hook) twice.

FRONT POST TREBLE CROCHET

(abbreviated FPtr)

YO twice, insert hook from **front** to **back** around post of st indicated *(Fig. 6, page 156)*, YO and pull up a loop (4 loops on hook), (YO and draw through 2 loops on hook) 3 times.

BACKPACK

With smaller size hook, ch 51.

Rnd 1: Dc in third ch from hook and in next 47 chs, 4 dc in last ch; working in free loops of beginning ch *(Fig. 3b, page 155)*, dc in next 48 chs, 4 dc in last ch; join with slip st to top of beginning ch: 104 dc.

Rnd 2 (Right side): Ch 2 **(does not count as a st, now and throughout)**, turn; work FPdc around each of next 2 dc, † skip next 2 dc, work FPtr around each of next 2 dc, working **behind** 2 FPtr just made, work FPtr around each of 2 skipped dc, skip next 2 dc, work FPtr around each of next 2 dc, working in **front** of 2 FPtr just made, work FPtr around each of 2 skipped dc †; repeat from † to † 5 times **more**, work FPdc around each of next 4 dc, repeat from † to † around to last 2 dc, work FPdc around each of last 2 dc; join with slip st to first FPdc.

Note: Loop a short piece of yarn around any stitch to mark Rnd 2 as **right** side.

Rnd 3: Ch 2, turn; work BPdc around next st and each st around; join with slip st to first BPdc.

Rnd 4: Ch 2, turn; work FPdc around each of next 2 BPdc, † skip next 2 BPdc, work FPtr around each of next 2 BPdc, working in **front** of 2 FPtr just made, work FPtr around each of 2 skipped BPdc, skip next 2 BPdc, work FPtr around each of next 2 BPdc, working **behind** 2 FPtr just made, work FPtr around each of 2 skipped BPdc †; repeat from † to † 5 times **more**, work FPdc around each of next 4 BPdc, repeat from † to † around to last 2 BPdc, work FPdc around each of last 2 BPdc; join with slip st to first FPdc.

Rnd 5: Ch 2, turn; work BPdc around next st and each st around; join with slip st to first BPdc.

Rnd 6: Ch 2, turn; work FPdc around each of next 2 BPdc, † skip next 2 BPdc, work FPtr around each of next 2 BPdc, working **behind** 2 FPtr just made, work FPtr around each of 2 skipped BPdc, skip next 2 BPdc, work FPtr around each of next 2 BPdc, working in **front** of 2 FPtr just made, work FPtr around each of 2 skipped BPdc †; repeat from † to † 5 times **more**, work FPdc around each of next 4 BPdc, repeat from † to † around to last 2 BPdc, work FPdc around each of last 2 BPdc; join with slip st to first FPdc.

Rnds 7-29: Repeat Rnds 3-6, 5 times; then repeat Rnds 3-5 once **more**.

Rnd 30: Ch 2, turn; work FPdc around next st and each st around; join with slip st to first FPdc.

Rnd 31 (Eyelet rnd)**:** Ch 2, turn; work BPdc around each of next 5 FPdc, † ch 2, skip next 2 FPdc, work BPdc around each of next 6 FPdc †; repeat from † to † 4 times **more**, ch 2, skip next 2 FPdc, work BPdc around each of next 10 FPdc, repeat from † to † 5 times, ch 2, skip next 2 FPdc, work BPdc around each of last 5 FPdc; join with slip st to first BPdc: 12 ch-2 sps.

Rnd 32: Ch 2, turn; work FPdc around each of next 5 BPdc, † 2 hdc in next ch-2 sp, work FPdc around each of next 6 BPdc †; repeat from † to † 4 times **more**, 2 hdc in next ch-2 sp, work FPdc around each of next 10 BPdc, repeat from † to † around to last ch-2 sp, 2 hdc in last ch-2 sp, work FPdc around each of last 5 BPdc; join with slip st to first FPdc.

Rnd 33: Ch 2, turn; work BPdc around next st and each st around; join with slip st to first BPdc, finish off.

FINISHING

Optional Lining
Using Backpack as a guide and adding ½" (12 mm) seam allowances, cut fabric needed for inside of Backpack, then cut a 7" wide x 12" high (18 cm x 30.5 cm) piece from remaining fabric for pocket. Turn raw edges of pocket to **wrong** side ¼" (7 mm) twice, then sew close to edges. With **right** sides of pocket and lining fabric facing, sew pocket to one side of lining approximately 1¾" (4.5 cm) from top raw edge. Divide pocket into desired sections by sewing seams from top to bottom of pocket. With **right** side of lining fabric together, sew side and bottom seams. Turn raw edges of lining to **wrong** side, then hand sew lining to inside of Backpack to top of Rnd 29.

Strap *(Make 2)*
Using larger size hook, macrame cord, and leaving a 1" (30.5 cm) end for knotting at each end, make a 66" (167.5 cm) long chain, making sure that both Straps are the same length.

Finish off.

Beginning at one side edge, weave one Strap through Eyelet Rnd, ending at same side edge.

Beginning at opposite side edge, weave remaining Strap through Eyelet Rnd in same manner.

Hold together both long ends of one Strap and make an overhand knot as close as possible to chains. With smaller size hook, pull long ends of Strap through bottom corner at same side of Backpack. Tie an overhand knot with long ends as close as possible to corner.

Thread 4 beads as desired onto each long end and make an overhand knot below bottom bead on each end. Trim ends.

Repeat with opposite Strap.

DESIGNED BY
Melissa Leapman

Reversible Scarf

■■□□ **EASY**

Finished Measurements:

7½" wide x 80" long (19 cm x 203 cm)

SHOPPING LIST

- **Yarn** (Medium Weight) **4**
  [3.5 ounces, 170 yards
  (100 grams, 156 meters) per skein]:
  - Blue - 2 skeins
  - Taupe - 2 skeins

- **Crochet Hook**
  - Size I (5.5 mm) **or** size needed
    for gauge

Gauge Information:

Gauge Swatch:
7½" wide x 4" high
(19 cm x 10 cm)

Work same as Scarf, page 112,
for 12 rows; do **not** finish off:
23 hdc.

STITCH GUIDE

LONG DOUBLE CROCHET
(abbreviated Ldc)

YO, insert hook in sc in row **below** next hdc, YO and pull up a loop even with last st made, (YO and draw through 2 loops on hook) twice **(Fig. A)**.

Fig. A

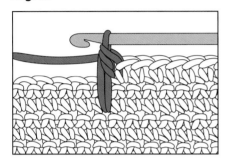

SCARF

With Blue, ch 24.

Row 1: Sc in second ch from hook and in each ch across: 23 sts.

When changing colors **(Fig. 5b, page 155)**, do **not** cut yarn, carry unused yarn **loosely** along edge.

Row 2: Ch 2 (**counts as first hdc, now and throughout**), turn; hdc in next sc and in each sc across, changing to Taupe in last hdc made.

Row 3: Ch 1, turn; sc in first 3 hdc, (work Ldc, sc in next 3 hdc) across.

Row 4: Ch 2, turn; hdc in next sc and in each st across, changing to Blue in last hdc made.

Row 5: Ch 1, turn; sc in first hdc, work Ldc, (sc in next 3 hdc, work Ldc) across to last hdc, sc in last hdc.

Row 6: Ch 2, turn; hdc in next st and in each st across, changing to Taupe in last hdc made.

Repeat Rows 3-6 for pattern until Scarf measures approximately 80" (203 cm) from beginning ch, ending by working Row 6; at end of last row, do **not** change colors; cut Taupe and finish off Blue.

DESIGNED BY
Melissa Leapman

Shawlette

 **EASY**

Finished Measurements:

68" long x 10½" wide (172.5 cm x 26.5 cm)

SHOPPING LIST

- **Yarn** (Medium Weight) 〔4〕
  [3.5 ounces, 270 yards
  (100 grams, 247 meters) per skein]:
  - 2 skeins

- **Crochet Hook**
  - Size I (5.5 mm) **or** size needed
    for gauge

Gauge Information:

18 dc and 8 rows = 4" (10 cm)

Gauge Swatch:
4" (10 cm) square

Ch 20.

Row 1: Dc in fourth ch from hook **(3 skipped chs count as first dc)** and in each ch across: 18 dc.

Rows 2-8: Ch 3 **(counts as first dc)**, turn; dc in next dc and in each dc across.

Finish off.

STITCH GUIDE

DOUBLE CROCHET 2 TOGETHER
(abbreviated dc2tog)
(uses next 2 dc)

★ YO, insert hook in **next** dc, YO and pull up a loop, YO and draw through 2 loops on hook; repeat from ★ once **more**, YO and draw through all 3 loops on hook **(counts as one dc)**.

WRAP

Ch 13, place marker in third ch from hook for st placement.

Row 1: Dc in eighth ch from hook and in next ch, ch 3, skip next 3 chs, 4 dc in last ch: 6 dc and 2 sps.

Row 2 (Right side): Ch 3, turn; slip st in first dc, ch 2, hdc in next dc, ch 2, hdc in next 2 dc, ch 3, dc in next 2 dc, ch 2, 2 dc in marked ch, remove marker: 7 sts and 5 sps.

Row 3: Ch 3 **(counts as first dc)**, turn; dc in next dc, ch 2, dc in next 2 dc, ch 3, skip next ch-3 sp, (3 dc, ch 1, 3 dc) in next ch-2 sp, leave remaining sts unworked: 10 dc and 3 sps.

Row 4: Ch 3, turn; slip st in first dc, ch 2, hdc in next 2 dc, ch 2, hdc in next 3 dc, ch 3, dc in next 2 dc, ch 2, dc in next dc, 2 dc in last dc: 10 sts and 5 sps.

Row 5: Ch 3 **(counts as first dc)**, turn; dc in next 2 dc, ch 2, dc in next 2 dc, ch 3, skip next ch-3 sp, (3 dc, ch 1, 3 dc) in next ch-2 sp, leave remaining sts unworked: 11 dc and 3 sps.

Row 6: Ch 3, turn; slip st in first dc, ch 2, hdc in next 2 dc, ch 2, hdc in next 3 dc, ch 3, dc in next 2 dc, ch 2, dc in next 2 dc, 2 dc in last dc: 11 sts and 5 sps.

Row 7: Ch 3 **(counts as first dc)**, turn; dc in next dc and in each dc across to next ch-2 sp, ch 2, dc in next 2 dc, ch 3, skip next ch-3 sp, (3 dc, ch 1, 3 dc) in next ch-2 sp, leave remaining sts unworked: 12 dc and 3 sps.

Row 8 (Increase row): Ch 3, turn; slip st in first dc, ch 2, hdc in next 2 dc, ch 2, hdc in next 3 dc, ch 3, dc in next 2 dc, ch 2, dc in next dc and in each dc across to last dc, 2 dc in last dc: 12 sts and 5 sps.

Rows 9-69: Repeat Rows 7 and 8, 30 times; then repeat Row 7 once **more**: 43 dc and 3 sps.

Row 70 (Decrease row): Ch 3, turn; slip st in first dc, ch 2, hdc in next 2 dc, ch 2, hdc in next 3 dc, ch 3, dc in next 2 dc, ch 2, dc in next dc and in each dc across to last 2 dc, dc2tog: 41 sts and 5 sps.

Row 71: Ch 3 **(counts as first dc)**, turn; dc in next dc and in each dc across to next ch-2 sp, ch 2, dc in next 2 dc, ch 3, (3 dc, ch 1, 3 dc) in next ch-2 sp, leave remaining sts unworked: 42 dc and 3 sps.

Rows 72-135: Repeat Rows 70 and 71, 32 times: 10 dc and 3 sps.

Row 136: Ch 3, turn; slip st in first dc, ch 2, hdc in next 2 dc, ch 2, hdc in next 3 dc, ch 3, dc in next 2 dc, ch 2, dc2tog; finish off.

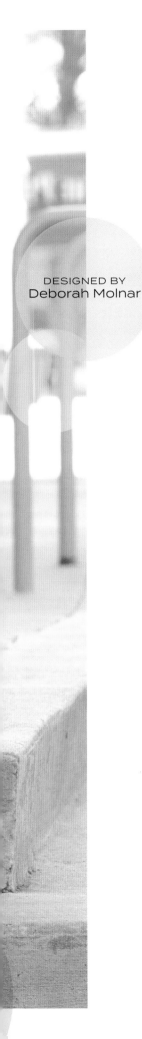

DESIGNED BY
Deborah Molnar

Versatility Set

■■□□ **EASY**

Finished Measurements:

Cuff

5½" high x 12½" circumference
(14 cm x 32 cm)

Ear Warmer

4" wide x 18½" circumference
(10 cm x 47 cm)

SHOPPING LIST

- **Yarn** (Medium Weight) 🧶**4**
  [7 ounces, 364 yards
  (198 grams, 333 meters) per skein]:
  - Tan - 1 skein
  - Black - 10 yards (9 meters)

- **Crochet Hooks**
  - Size L (8 mm) **or** size needed
    for gauge
  - Size H (5 mm)

- **Additional Supplies**
  - Yarn needle

Gauge Information:

With larger size hook and
holding two strands of
yarn together, 9 dc and
6 rows/rnds = 4" (10 cm)

Gauge Swatch:

4" (10 cm) square

With larger size hook and
holding two strands of Tan
together, ch 11.

Row 1: Dc in fourth ch from
hook and in each ch across
**(3 skipped chs count as first
dc)**: 9 dc.

Rows 2-6: Ch 3 **(counts as
first dc)**, turn; dc in next dc
and in each dc across.

Finish off.

STITCH GUIDE

TREBLE CROCHET
(abbreviated tr)

YO twice, insert hook in st indicated, YO and pull up a loop (4 loops on hook), (YO and draw through 2 loops on hook) 3 times.

CUFF *(Make 2)*

Beginning at bottom edge, with larger size hook and holding two strands of Tan together, ch 28; being careful not to twist ch, join with slip st to form a ring.

Rnd 1 (Right side): Ch 3 **(counts as first dc, now and throughout)**, dc in next ch and in each ch around; join with slip st to first dc: 28 dc.

Note: Loop a short piece of yarn around any stitch to mark Rnd 1 as **right** side.

Rnds 2-7: Ch 3, dc in next dc and in each dc around; join with slip st to first dc.

Rnd 8: Ch 1; working from **left** to **right**, work reverse sc in each dc around *(Figs. 9a-d, page 156)*; join with slip st to first st, finish off.

BOW *(Make 2)*

With smaller size hook, using one strand of Black, and leaving a long end, ch 3; join with slip st to form a ring.

Rnd 1 (Right side): Ch 1, work (sc, hdc, dc, tr, dc, hdc, sc, ch 1) twice in ring; join with slip st to first sc, finish off leaving a 12" (30.5 cm) end.

Note: Mark Rnd 1 as **right** side.

Wrap the long end around the center of the Bow several times to form the knot; then tie the yarn ends in a knot on the **wrong** side of the Bow. Thread yarn needle with the ends and using photo as a guide for placement, sew Bow to **right** side of Cuff.

EAR WARMER

With larger size hook and holding two strands of Tan together, ch 42; being careful **not** to twist ch, join with slip st to form a ring.

Rnd 1 (Right side): Ch 3 **(counts as first dc, now and throughout)**, dc in next ch and in each ch around; join with slip st to first dc: 42 dc.

Note: Mark Rnd 1 as **right** side.

Rnds 2-4: Ch 3, dc in next dc and in each dc around; join with slip st to first dc.

Rnd 5: Ch 1; working from **left** to **right**, work reverse sc in each dc around; join with slip st to first st, finish off.

Edging: With **right** side facing, holding two strands of Tan together, and working in free loops of beginning ch *(Fig. 3b, page 155)*, join yarn with slip st in same ch as joining slip st; working from **left** to **right**, work reverse sc in each ch around; join with slip st to first st, finish off.

Bow
Work same as Cuff Bow, page 120; thread yarn needle with the ends and sew to **right** side of Ear Warmer.

VERSATILITY SET OPTIONS

Note: Each Option set uses an amount of yarn that is slightly less than the Tan set.

Option #1: Crochet the set using one strand **each** of Red and Black, working through Rnd 7 on the Cuffs and Rnd 4 on the Ear Warmer.

Option #2: Crochet the set using two strands of Green, working through Rnd 7 of the Cuff and through Rnd 4 of the Ear Warmer. Use buttons in place of the Bows.

Option #3: Crochet the set using two strands of Maroon, working in Back Loops Only of each stitch through Rnd 7 on the Cuffs and through Rnd 4 of the Ear Warmer *(Fig. 4, page 155)*. Use buttons in place of the Bows.

Circles & Beads Necklace

DESIGNED BY
Edie Eckman

■■□□ **EASY**

Finished Measurement:

Approximately 40" (101.5 cm) circumference

SHOPPING LIST

- **Thread** (Lace Weight) 🧵 **0** LACE
  [350 yards (320 meters) per ball]:
  - 1 ball

- **Steel Crochet Hook**
  - Size 2 (2.25 mm)

- **Additional Supplies**
  - 40" (101.5 cm) length Suede lace cord
  - 8 mm silver spacer - 30 beads with large holes
  - Fold-over cord ends - 2
  - Craft glue
  - Jump rings - 2
  - Lobster clasp - 1
  - Chain-nose pliers (2 pair)

Gauge Information:

Each Circle Motif = $7/8$" (2 cm) diameter

Gauge Swatch:
Not crucial in this project.

CIRCLE MOTIF *(Make 25)*

Ch 6; join with slip st to form a ring.

Rnd 1 (Right side): Ch 3 **(counts as first dc)**, 15 dc in ring; join with slip st to first dc, finish off.

FINISHING

Thread 3 beads onto cord; then alternately thread one circle motif and one bead, ending with 3 beads following last motif.

Lay one suede end in one fold-over cord end, apply a drop of glue, and use the chain-nose pliers to fold the tabs down over the suede end *(Fig. A)*.

Repeat with the opposite end of the suede. Join one jump ring and lobster clasp to one fold-over cord end and the remaining jump ring to the other fold-over cord end.

Fig. A

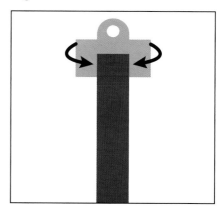

Cabled Handbag

DESIGNED BY
Bonnie Barker

▮▮▮▭ **INTERMEDIATE**

Finished Size:

10" wide x 10¼" deep (25.5 cm x 26 cm)
(excluding Handle Casing and Handles)

SHOPPING LIST

- **Yarn** (Medium Weight) 🏷️4
  [5 ounces, 251 yards
  (142 grams, 230 meters) per skein]:
  - Dk Green - 1 skein
  - Lt Green - 1 skein

- **Crochet Hook**
  - Size I (5.5 mm) **or** size needed for gauge

- **Additional Supplies**
  - 8⅛" x 4" (20.5 cm x 10 cm) pair of Handles
  - Yarn needle
  - ½ yard (.5 meter) Fabric for lining (recommended)
  - Sewing needle
  - Matching thread

Gauge Information:

In Body pattern,
16 sts and 8 rnds/rows = 4"
(10 cm)

Gauge Swatch:
4" (10 cm) square

With Lt Green, ch 17.

Row 1: Dc in third ch from hook **(2 skipped chs count as first dc)** and in each ch across: 16 dc.

Row 2: Ch 2 **(counts as first dc)**, turn; work BPdc around next st and each st across to last dc, dc in last dc.

Row 3: Ch 2 **(counts as first dc)**, turn; work FPdc around next BPdc and each BPdc across to last dc, dc in last dc.

Rows 4-8: Repeat Rows 2 and 3 twice, then repeat Row 2 once **more**.

Finish off.

STITCH GUIDE

BACK POST DOUBLE CROCHET
(abbreviated BPdc)

YO, insert hook from **back** to **front** around post of st indicated *(Fig. 6, page 156)*, YO and pull up a loop (3 loops on hook), (YO and draw through 2 loops on hook) twice.

FRONT POST DOUBLE CROCHET
(abbreviated FPdc)

YO, insert hook from **front** to **back** around post of st indicated *(Fig. 6, page 156)*, YO and pull up a loop (3 loops on hook), (YO and draw through 2 loops on hook) twice.

FRONT POST TREBLE CROCHET
(abbreviated FPtr)

YO twice, insert hook from **front** to **back** around post of st indicated *(Fig. 6, page 156)*, YO and pull up a loop (4 loops on hook), (YO and draw through 2 loops on hook) 3 times.

BODY

With Dk Green, ch 40.

Rnd 1: Dc in third ch from hook **(2 skipped chs do not count as a st)** and in each ch across to last ch, 4 dc in last ch; working in free loops of beginning ch *(Fig. 3b, page 155)*, dc in next ch and in each ch across to same ch as first dc, 3 dc in same ch; join with slip st to first dc: 80 dc.

Rnd 2 (Right side): Ch 2 **(does not count as a st, now and throughout Body)**, turn; ★ skip next 2 dc, work FPtr around next 2 dc, working in **front** of FPtr just made, work FPtr around 2 skipped dc; repeat from ★ around; join with slip st to first FPtr: 20 Cables.

Note: Loop a short piece of yarn around any stitch to mark Rnd 2 as **right** side.

Rnd 3: Ch 2, turn; work BPdc around next FPtr and each FPtr around; join with slip st to first BPdc: 80 BPdc.

Rnd 4: Ch 2, turn; ★ skip next 2 BPdc, work FPtr around next 2 BPdc, working in **front** of FPtr just made, work FPtr around 2 skipped BPdc; repeat from ★ around; join with slip st to first FPtr changing to Lt Green *(Fig. 5d, page 155)*, cut Dk Green.

Rnd 5: Ch 2, turn; work BPdc around next FPtr and each FPtr around; join with slip st to first BPdc.

Rnd 6: Ch 3 **(does not count as a st, now and throughout)**, turn; skip next 4 BPdc, work FPtr around next 2 BPdc, working in **front** of FPtr just made, work FPtr around third and fourth skipped BPdc, ★ skip next 2 BPdc, work FPtr around next 2 BPdc, working in **front** of FPtr just made, work FPtr around 2 skipped BPdc; repeat from ★ around ending by working around first 2 skipped BPdc; join with slip st to first FPtr.

Rnd 7: Ch 2, turn; work BPdc around next FPtr and each FPtr around; join with slip st to first BPdc.

Rnd 8: Ch 2, turn; ★ skip next 2 BPdc, work FPtr around next 2 BPdc, working in **front** of FPtr just made, work FPtr around 2 skipped BPdc; repeat from ★ around; join with slip st to first FPtr changing to Dk Green, cut Lt Green.

Rnds 9 and 10: Repeat Rnds 5 and 6.

Rnds 11 and 12: Repeat Rnds 3 and 4.

Rnds 13-19: Repeat Rnds 5-11.

Rnd 20: Ch 2, turn; ★ skip next 2 BPdc, work FPtr around next 2 BPdc, working in **front** of FPtr just made, work FPtr around 2 skipped BPdc; repeat from ★ around; join with slip st to first FPtr.

Rnd 21: Ch 1, do **not** turn; sc in first 8 FPtr, work FPdc around next 24 FPtr, sc in next 16 FPtr, work FPdc around next 24 FPtr, sc in last 8 FPtr; join with slip st to first sc, finish off.

HANDLE CASING

First Side

Row 1: With **right** side facing, skip first 7 sc on Rnd 21 and join Dk Green with slip st in next sc; ch 2 **(counts as first dc, now and throughout)**, work FPdc around next 24 FPdc, dc in next sc, leave remaining sts unworked: 26 sts.

Row 2: Ch 2, turn; work BPdc around next 24 FPdc, dc in last dc.

Row 3: Ch 2, turn; work FPdc around next 24 BPdc, dc in last dc.

Rows 4-6: Repeat Rows 2 and 3 once, then repeat Row 2 once **more**; at end of Row 6, finish off leaving 20" (51 cm) strand for sewing Handle Casing.

Second Side

Row 1: With **right** side facing, skip next 14 sc from First Side and join Dk Green with slip st in next sc; ch 2, work FPdc around next 24 FPdc, dc in next sc, leave remaining sts unworked: 26 sts.

Rows 2-6: Work same as First Side.

Thread yarn needle with long end from either Handle Casing. Fold Handle Casing over one handle and sew sts on Row 6 to sts on Rnd 19 of Body.

Repeat with remaining Handle.

LINING

Using Bag as a guide and adding ½" (12 mm) seam allowances, cut fabric needed for inside of Bag excluding Handle Casings and last 2 rnds of Body. With **right** side of fabric together, sew side seams of Bag lining. Turn raw edges of lining to **wrong** side, then hand sew lining to inside of Bag along seams of Handle Casings and across the top of Rnd 19.

DESIGNED BY
Bonnie Barker

Cabled Set

 **EASY+**

Finished Measurements:

Cap: Fits 20" (51 cm) head circumference

Mitt: 7½" long x 8½" circumference
(19 cm x 21.5 cm)

Cowl: 6" high x 27" circumference
(15 cm x 68.5 cm)

SHOPPING LIST

- **Yarn** (Medium Weight)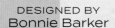
  [5 ounces, 256 yards
  (141 grams, 234 meters) per skein]:
  - 3 skeins
- **Crochet Hooks**
  - Size I (5.5 mm) **and**
  - Size J (6 mm) **or** sizes needed
    for gauge

Gauge Information:

Mitts

With smaller size hook, in
pattern, 16 sts = 4¼" (10.75 cm);
10 rows/rnds = 4" (10 cm)

Cap and Cowl

With larger size hook, in
pattern, 16 sts = 4½" (11.5 cm);
9 rows/rnds = 4" (10 cm)

Gauge Swatch:
4¼" wide x 4" high
(10.75 cm x 10 cm)

With smaller size hook, ch 18.

Row 1: Dc in third ch from
hook and in each ch across:
16 dc.

Row 2: Ch 2 **(does not count
as a st, now and throughout)**,
turn; skip first 2 sts, † work
FPtr around next 2 sts,
working in **front** of FPtr just
made, work FPtr around
2 skipped sts, work FPdc
around next 4 sts †, skip next
2 sts, repeat from † to † once.

Row 3: Ch 2, turn; work BPdc
around each st across.

Row 4: Ch 2, turn; work FPdc around first 4 sts, † skip next 2 sts, work FPtr around next 2 sts, working in **front** of FPtr just made, work FPtr around 2 skipped sts †, work FPdc around next 4 sts, repeat from † to † once.

Row 5: Ch 2, turn; work BPdc around each st across.

Rows 6-10: Repeat Rows 2-5 once, then repeat Row 2 once **more**.

Finish off.

STITCH GUIDE

FRONT POST DOUBLE CROCHET
(abbreviated FPdc)

YO, insert hook from **front** to **back** around post of st indicated *(Fig. 6, page 156)*, YO and pull up a loop (3 loops on hook), (YO and draw through 2 loops on hook) twice.

BACK POST DOUBLE CROCHET
(abbreviated BPdc)

YO, insert hook from **back** to **front** around post of st indicated *(Fig. 6, page 156)*, YO and pull up a loop (3 loops on hook), (YO and draw through 2 loops on hook) twice.

FRONT POST TREBLE CROCHET
(abbreviated FPtr)

YO twice, insert hook from **front** to **back** around post of st indicated *(Fig. 6, page 156)*, YO and pull up a loop (4 loops on hook), (YO and draw through 2 loops on hook) 3 times.

CABLE

Ch 3, skip next 2 sc, sc in next sc, **turn**; sc in next 3 chs, slip st in next sc (Cable made), **turn**; working **behind** Cable, sc in 2 skipped sc *(Figs. A-E)*.

Fig. A

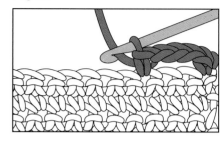

Fig. B

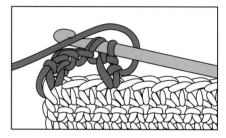

Fig. C

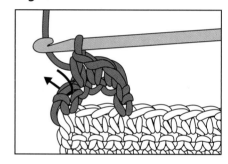

Fig. D

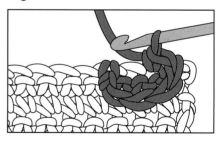

Fig. E

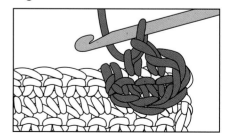

CAP

With larger size hook, ch 4; join with slip st to form a ring.

Rnd 1 (Right side)**:** Ch 1, 9 sc in ring; join with slip st to first sc.

Rnds 2 and 3: Ch 1, 2 sc in same st as joining and in each sc around; join with slip st to first sc: 36 sc.

Rnd 4: Ch 1, sc in same st as joining and in next sc, 2 sc in next sc, (sc in next 2 sc, 2 sc in next sc) around; join with slip st to first sc: 48 sc.

Rnd 5: Ch 2 **(does not count as a st, now and throughout)**, dc in same st as joining, 2 dc in next sc, (dc in next sc, 2 dc in next sc) around; skip beginning ch-2 **(now and throughout)** and join with slip st to first dc: 72 dc.

Rnd 6: Ch 2, skip first 2 dc, ★ † work FPtr around next 2 dc, working in **front** of FPtr just made, work FPtr around 2 skipped dc, work FPdc around next 4 dc †, skip next 2 dc; repeat from ★ 7 times **more**, then repeat from † to † once; join with slip st to first FPtr.

Rnd 7: Ch 2, turn; work BPdc around first st and each st around; join with slip st to first BPdc.

Rnd 8: Ch 2, turn; work FPdc around first 4 BPdc, ★ † skip next 2 BPdc, work FPtr around next 2 BPdc, working in **front** of FPtr just made, work FPtr around 2 skipped BPdc †, work FPdc around next 4 BPdc; repeat from ★ 7 times **more**, then repeat from † to † once; join with slip st to first FPdc.

Rnd 9: Ch 2, turn; work BPdc around first st and each st around; join with slip st to first BPdc.

Rnd 10: Ch 2, turn; skip first 2 BPdc, ★ † work FPtr around next 2 BPdc, working in **front** of FPtr just made, work FPtr around 2 skipped BPdc, work FPdc around next 4 BPdc †, skip next 2 BPdc; repeat from ★ 7 times **more**, then repeat from † to † once; join with slip st to first FPtr.

Rnds 11-19: Repeat Rnds 7-10 twice, then repeat Rnd 7 once **more**.

Rnd 20: Ch 1, turn; working in Front Loops Only **(Fig. 4, page 155)**, slip st in each st around; join with slip st to **both** loops of first slip st.

Rnd 21: Ch 1, turn; working in free loops of Rnd 19 **(Fig. 3a, page 155)**, sc in each st around; join with slip st to first sc.

Rnd 22: Ch 1, turn; sc in first sc, work Cables around to last 2 sc, ch 3, skip last 2 sc, slip st in first sc made on rnd, **turn;** sc in next 3 chs, slip st in next sc (last Cable made), **turn;** working **behind** Cable, sc in 2 skipped sc; join with slip st to last slip st made: 24 Cables and 48 sc **behind** Cables.

Rnd 23: Ch 1, turn; working in sc **behind** Cables only, (sc in next sc, 2 sc in next sc) around; join with slip st to first sc: 72 sc.

Rnd 24: Ch 1, turn; working in Front Loops Only, slip st in each sc around; join with slip st to **both** loops of first slip st.

Rnd 25: Ch 1, turn; working in free loops of Rnd 23, sc in each st around; join with slip st to first sc.

Rnd 26: Ch 1, turn; slip st in each sc around; join with slip st to first slip st, finish off.

MITT *(Make 2)*

With smaller size hook, ch 30; being careful **not** to twist ch, join with slip st to form a ring.

Rnd 1: Ch 1, sc in same ch as joining and in each ch around; join with slip st to first sc: 30 sc.

Rnd 2 (Right side)**:** Ch 1, turn; working in Front Loops Only, slip st in each sc around; join with slip st to **both** loops of first slip st.

Rnd 3: Ch 1, turn; working in free loops of previous rnd, sc in each st around; join with slip st to first sc.

Rnd 4: Ch 1, turn; sc in first sc, work Cables around to last 2 sc, ch 3, skip last 2 sc, slip st in first sc made on rnd, **turn**; sc in next 3 chs, slip st in next sc (last Cable made), **turn**; sc in 2 skipped sc; join with slip st to last slip st made: 10 Cables and 20 sc **behind** Cables.

Rnd 5: Ch 1, turn; working in sc **behind** Cables only, (2 sc in next sc, sc in next sc) around; join with slip st to first sc: 30 sc.

Rnds 6 and 7: Repeat Rnds 2 and 3.

Rnd 8: Ch 2, do **not** turn; 2 dc in first sc, dc in next sc and in each sc around to last sc, 2 dc in last sc; join with slip st to first dc: 32 dc.

Rnd 9: Ch 2, turn; skip first 2 sts, ★ † work FPtr around next 2 sts, working in **front** of FPtr just made, work FPtr around 2 skipped sts, work FPdc around next 4 sts †, skip next 2 sts; repeat from ★ 2 times **more**, then repeat from † to † once; join with slip st to first FPtr.

Rnd 10: Ch 2, turn; work BPdc around first st and each st around; join with slip st to first BPdc.

Rnd 11: Ch 2, turn; work FPdc around first 4 BPdc, ★ † skip next 2 BPdc, work FPtr around next 2 BPdc, working in **front** of FPtr just made, work FPtr around 2 skipped BPdc †, work FPdc around next 4 BPdc; repeat from ★ 2 times **more**, then repeat from † to † once; join with slip st to first FPdc.

Rnd 12: Ch 2, turn; work BPdc around first st and each st around; join with slip st to first BPdc.

Rnds 13-15: Repeat Rnds 9-11.

Rnd 16: Ch 2, turn; work BPdc around first st and each st around to last 4 sts, ch 4, skip last 4 sts (thumb opening); join with slip st to first BPdc: 28 sts and one ch-4 sp.

Rnd 17: Ch 2, turn; 4 dc in first ch-4 sp, work FPdc around next 4 BPdc, ★ skip next 2 BPdc, work FPtr around next 2 BPdc, working in **front** of FPtr just made, work FPtr around 2 skipped BPdc, work FPdc around next 4 BPdc; repeat from ★ around; join with slip st to first dc.

Rnds 18-20: Repeat Rnds 10-12.

Rnd 21: Ch 1, turn; slip st in each st around; join with slip st to joining slip st, finish off.

COWL

With larger size hook, ch 96; being careful **not** to twist ch, join with slip st to form a ring.

Rnd 1: Ch 1, sc in same ch as joining and in each ch around; join with slip st to first sc: 96 sc.

Rnd 2 (Right side): Ch 1, turn; working in Front Loops Only, slip st in each sc around; join with slip st to first slip st.

Rnd 3: Ch 1, turn; working in free loops of previous rnd, sc in each st around; join with slip st to first sc.

Rnd 4: Ch 1, turn; sc in first sc, work Cables around to last 2 sc, ch 3, skip last 2 sc, slip st in first sc made on rnd, **turn**; sc in next 3 chs, slip st in next sc (last Cable made), **turn**; sc in 2 skipped sc; join with slip st to last slip st made: 32 Cables and 64 sc **behind** Cables.

Rnd 5: Ch 1, turn; working in sc **behind** Cables only, (2 sc in next sc, sc in next sc) around; join with slip st to first sc: 96 sc.

Rnd 6: Ch 1, turn; working in Front Loops Only, slip st in each sc around; join with slip st to both loops of first slip st.

Rnd 7: Ch 2, turn; working in free loops of Rnd 5, dc in first sc and in each sc around; join with slip st to first dc.

Rnd 8: Ch 2, turn; skip first 2 sts, ★ † work FPtr around next 2 sts, working in **front** of FPtr just made, work FPtr around 2 skipped sts, work FPdc around next 4 sts †, skip next 2 sts; repeat from ★ 10 times **more**, then repeat from † to † once; join with slip st to first FPtr.

Rnd 9: Ch 2, turn; work BPdc around first st and each st around; join with slip st to first BPdc.

Rnd 10: Ch 2, turn; work FPdc around first 4 sts, ★ † skip next 2 sts, work FPtr around next 2 sts, working in **front** of FPtr just made, work FPtr around 2 skipped sts †, work FPdc around next 4 sts; repeat from ★ 10 times **more**, then repeat from † to † once; join with slip st to first FPdc.

Rnd 11: Ch 2, turn; work BPdc around first st and each st around; join with slip st to first BPdc.

Rnds 12-15: Repeat Rnds 8-11.

Rnd 16: Ch 1, turn; working in Front Loops Only, slip st in each st around; join with slip st to **both** loops of first slip st.

Rnds 17-20: Repeat Rnds 3-6.

Rnd 21: Ch 1, turn; working in free loops of Rnd 19, sc in each st around; join with slip st to first sc.

Rnd 22: Ch 1, turn; slip st in each sc around; join with slip st to first slip st, finish off.

Cameo Bracelet

 **EASY**

Finished Measurements:

⅞" wide x 7½" long (22 mm x 19 cm) (excluding clasp)

DESIGNED BY
Kristen
Stoltzfus Clay

SHOPPING LIST

- **Thread** (Lace Weight) **0** LACE
  [350 yards (320 meters) per ball]:
  15 yards (13.5 meters)

- **Steel Crochet Hook**
  - Size 7 (1.65 mm)

- **Additional Supplies**
  - Flexible wire beading needle
  - Silver-tone toggle clasp
  - 14 mm flat oval stone beads - 5

Gauge Information:

Each Motif = approximately
1¼" long x ⅞" wide (3.25 cm x 22 mm)

Gauge Swatch:
Not crucial in this project; use any size steel crochet hook needed to achieve desired look.

STITCH GUIDE

TREBLE CROCHET
(abbreviated tr)

YO twice, insert hook in sp indicated, YO and pull up a loop (4 loops on hook), (YO and draw through 2 loops on hook) 3 times.

MOTIF *(Make 5)*

Leaving a long end for sewing, ch 6; join with slip st to form a ring.

Rnd 1 (Right side)**:** Ch 1, (5 hdc, dc, tr, dc) twice in ring; join with slip st to first hdc: 10 hdc, 4 dc, and 2 tr.

Note: Loop a short piece of thread around any stitch to mark Rnd 1 as **right** side.

Rnd 2: Ch 1, sc in same st as joining and in next 5 sts, 3 hdc in next tr, sc in next 7 sts, 3 hdc in next tr, sc in last dc; join with slip st to first sc: 20 sts.

Rnd 3: ★ (Ch 3, dc) in same st, skip next st, slip st in next st; repeat from ★ around, ending by working last slip st in same st as joining slip st, finish off.

FINISHING

See Finishing Components, page 158.

Using photo as a guide for placement and long ends, sew one bead to right side of each Motif.

Sew Motifs together, working through third ch of ch-3 at ends of Motifs, forming a strip. Sew half of toggle clasp to each end.

DESIGNED BY
Lisa Gentry

Kid Stuff

 **EASY**

Finished Measurements:

Fits Head Circumference:
Small - 15¾" (40 cm)
Large - 17" (43 cm)

Size Note: We have printed the instructions for the sizes in different colors to make it easier for you to find:

Small size = PINK
Large size = GREEN
All sizes = BLACK

Gauge Information:

Rnds 1-4 = 4¼" (10.75 cm);
14 sc = 4" (10 cm)

Gauge Swatch:
4¼" (10.75 cm) diameter

Work same as Hat, page 138, through Rnd 4; do **not** finish off.

SHOPPING LIST

▪ **Yarn** (Medium Weight)
[3.5 ounces, 207 yards
(100 grams, 188 meters) per skein]:
▪ MC (Purple) - 1 skein
▪ CC (Tan) - 1 skein

▪ **Crochet Hook**
▪ Size I (5.5 mm) **or** size needed for gauge

STITCH GUIDE

FRONT POST DOUBLE CROCHET
(abbreviated FPdc)

YO, insert hook from **front** to **back** around post of st indicated *(Fig. 6, page 156)*, YO and pull up a loop even with loop on hook (3 loops on hook), (YO and draw through 2 loops on hook) twice.

DOUBLE CROCHET 2 TOGETHER
(abbreviated dc2tog)

★ YO, insert hook in **next** st, YO and pull up a loop, YO and draw through 2 loops on hook; repeat from ★ once **more**, YO and draw through all 3 loops on hook **(counts as one dc)**.

HAT

With MC, ch 4; join with slip st to form a ring.

Rnd 1 (Right side): Ch 3 **(counts as first dc, now and throughout)**, 10{11} dc in ring; join with slip st to first dc: 11{12} dc.

Rnd 2: Ch 3, work FPdc around same st, ★ dc in next dc, work FPdc around same st; repeat from ★ around; join with slip st to first dc changing to CC *(Fig. 5d, page 155)*; do **not** cut MC: 11{12} dc and 11{12} FPdc.

Rnd 3: Ch 3, dc in same st, work FPdc around next FPdc, ★ 2 dc in next dc, work FPdc around next FPdc; repeat from ★ around; join with slip st to first dc changing to MC; do **not** cut CC: 22{24} dc and 11{12} FPdc.

Rnd 4: Ch 3, 2 dc in next dc, work FPdc around next FPdc, ★ dc in next dc, 2 dc in next dc, work FPdc around next FPdc; repeat from ★ around; join with slip st to first dc: 33{36} dc and 11{12} FPdc.

Rnd 5: Ch 3, dc in next dc, 2 dc in next dc, work FPdc around next FPdc, ★ dc in next 2 dc, 2 dc in next dc, work FPdc around next FPdc; repeat from ★ around; join with slip st to first dc changing to CC; do **not** cut MC: 44{48} dc and 11{12} FPdc.

Rnd 6: Ch 3, dc in next 2 dc, 2 dc in next dc, work FPdc around next FPdc, ★ dc in next 3 dc, 2 dc in next dc, work FPdc around next FPdc; repeat from ★ around; join with slip st to first dc changing to MC; do **not** cut CC: 55{60} dc and 11{12} FPdc.

Rnd 7: Ch 3, dc in next 3 dc, 2 dc in next dc, work FPdc around next FPdc, ★ dc in next 4 dc, 2 dc in next dc, work FPdc around next FPdc; repeat from ★ around; join with slip st to first dc: 66{72} dc and 11{12} FPdc.

Rnd 8: Ch 3, dc in next 5 dc, work FPdc around next FPdc, ★ dc in next 6 dc, work FPdc around next FPdc; repeat from ★ around; join with slip st to first dc changing to CC; do **not** cut MC.

Rnd 9: Ch 3, dc in next 5 dc, work FPdc around next FPdc, ★ dc in next 6 dc, work FPdc around next FPdc; repeat from ★ around; join with slip st to first dc changing to MC; do **not** cut CC.

Rnd 10: Ch 3, dc in next 5 dc, work FPdc around next FPdc, ★ dc in next 6 dc, work FPdc around next FPdc; repeat from ★ around; join with slip st to first dc.

Rnds 11 and 12: Repeat Rnds 8 and 9.

Cut CC.

Rnd 13: Ch 3, dc2tog twice, dc in next dc, work FPdc around next FPdc, ★ dc in next dc, dc2tog twice, dc in next dc, work FPdc around next FPdc; repeat from ★ around; join with slip st to first dc: 44{48} dc and 11{12} FPdc.

Rnds 14-16: Ch 3, dc in next 3 dc, work FPdc around next FPdc, ★ dc in next 4 dc, work FPdc around next FPdc; repeat from ★ around; join with slip st to first dc.

Rnd 17 (Band): Ch 1, sc in same st as joining and in each st around; join with slip st to first sc, finish off.

Crocodile Stitch Tote

DESIGNED BY
Kristi Simpson

 **EASY**

Finished Measurements:

13" wide x 9½" high (33 cm x 24 cm)

SHOPPING LIST

- **Yarn** (Medium Weight) **4**
  [4 ounces, 212 yards
  (113 grams, 194 meters) per skein]:
  - Grey - 2 skeins

  [3.5 ounces, 147 yards
  (100 grams, 134 meters) per skein]:
  - Variegated - 1 skein

- **Crochet Hook**
  - Size H (5 mm) **or** size needed
    for gauge

- **Additional Supplies**
  - Yarn needle
  - Sewing needle
  - Matching thread
  - 1⅛" (29 mm) button

Gauge Information:

13 dc and 7 rows/rnds = 3½"
(9 cm)

Gauge Swatch:
3½" (9 cm) square

With Grey, ch 15.

Row 1: Dc in fourth ch from
hook **(3 skipped chs count
as first dc)** and in each ch
across: 13 dc.

Rows 2-7: Ch 3 **(counts as
first dc)**, turn; dc in next dc
and in each dc across.

Finish off.

STITCH GUIDE

DOUBLE CROCHET 2 TOGETHER
(abbreviated dc2tog)

★ YO, insert hook in **next** dc, YO
and pull up a loop, YO and draw
through 2 loops on hook; repeat
from ★ once **more**, YO and draw
through all 3 loops on hook
(counts as one dc).

BOTTOM

With Grey, ch 7.

Row 1 (Wrong side)**:** Working in back ridge of beginning ch *(Fig. 2, page 155)*, sc in second ch from hook and in each ch across: 6 sc.

Note: Loop a short piece of yarn around the back of any stitch on Row 1 to mark **right** side.

Rows 2-42: Ch 1, turn; sc in each sc across; at end of Row 42, do **not** finish off.

BODY

Rnd 1: Ch 2 **(does not count as a st, now and throughout)**, do **not** turn; dc in end of each row across; working in free loops of beginning ch *(Fig. 3b, page 155)*, dc in ch at base of first sc and in each ch across; dc in end of each row across; dc in first sc and in each sc on Row 42; skip beginning ch-2 **(now and throughout)** and join with slip st to first dc: 96 dc.

Rnds 2-7: Ch 2, dc in same st as joining and in each dc around; join with slip st to first dc.

Rnd 8: Ch 2, dc in same st as joining and in next 41 dc, dc2tog 3 times, dc in next dc and in each dc across to last 6 dc, dc2tog 3 times; join with slip st to first dc: 90 dc.

Rnd 9: Ch 2, dc in same st as joining and in each dc around; join with slip st to first dc.

Rnd 10: Ch 2, dc in same st as joining and in next 8 dc, dc2tog, (dc in next 13 dc, dc2tog) 5 times, dc in last 4 dc; join with slip st to first dc: 84 dc.

Rnds 11-13: Ch 2, dc in same st as joining and in each dc around; join with slip st to first dc.

Finish off.

Rnd 14: With **right** side facing, join Variegated with dc around post of first dc *(see Joining With Dc, page 154)*; work 3 dc down post of same dc *(Fig. A)*, ch 1, rotate piece *(Fig. B)* and work 4 dc up post of next dc to form a Scale *(Figs. C & D)*, skip next 2 dc, ★ work 4 dc down post of next dc, ch 1, rotate piece and work 4 dc up post of next dc, skip next 2 dc; repeat from ★ around; join with slip st to first dc: 21 Scales.

Fig. A

Fig. B

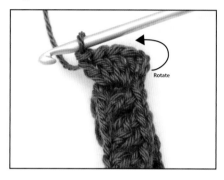

Fig. C

Fig. D

Rnd 15: Ch 2, slip st in center of first Scale, ch 3 **(counts as first dc, now and throughout)**, dc in same sp, working **around** previous rnd *(Fig. 7, page 156)*, 2 dc in sp **between** next 2 dc *(Fig. E)*, ★ 2 dc in center of next Scale, working **around** previous rnd, 2 dc in sp **between** next 2 dc; repeat from ★ around; join with slip st to first dc: 84 dc.

Fig. E

Rnd 16: Slip st in next 2 dc, ch 3, work 3 dc down post of same dc, ch 1, rotate piece and work 4 dc up post of next dc to form a Scale, skip next 2 dc, ★ 4 dc down post of next dc, ch 1, rotate piece and work 4 dc up post of next dc, skip next 2 sts; repeat from ★ around; join with slip st to first dc: 21 Scales.

Rnds 17 and 18: Repeat Rnds 15 and 16: 21 Scales.

Finish off.

Rnd 19: With **right** side facing, join Grey with dc in first dc on Rnd 17; dc in next 9 dc, dc2tog, (dc in next 10 dc, dc2tog) around; join with slip st to first dc: 77 dc.

Rnd 20: Ch 2, dc in same st as joining and in next 8 dc, dc2tog, (dc in next 9 dc, dc2tog) around; join with slip st to first dc: 70 dc.

Rnd 21: Ch 2, dc in same st as joining and in next 7 dc, dc2tog, (dc in next 8 dc, dc2tog) around; join with slip st to first dc: 63 dc.

Rnd 22: Ch 1, sc in same st as joining in next 17 dc, (slip st, ch 12, slip st) in next dc (button loop made), sc in each dc around; join with slip st to first sc, finish off.

Sew button to Body opposite button loop.

HANDLE *(Make 2)*

With Grey, ch 71.

Row 1: Sc in back ridge of second ch from hook and each ch across: 70 sc.

Row 2: Ch 2, turn; dc in first sc and in each sc across.

Row 3: Ch 1, turn; sc in each dc across; finish off.

Using photo as a guide for placement, sew Handles to Rnd 19 on front and back, spacing ends 5" (12.5 cm) apart.

Two-Way Button-Up Cowl

 **EASY**

Finished Measurements:

7" high x 28" long (18 cm x 71 cm)

SHOPPING LIST

- **Yarn** (Medium Weight) 4
  [3.5 ounces, 170 yards
  (100 grams, 156 meters) per skein]:
  - 1 skein

- **Crochet Hook**
  - Size I (5.5 mm) **or** size needed
    for gauge

- **Additional Supplies**
  - 1⅜" (35 mm) Buttons - 3
  - Sewing needle & matching thread

Gauge Information:

In pattern,
2 repeats = 4½" (11.5 cm)

Gauge Swatch:

7" wide x 4½" high
(17.75 cm x 11.5 cm)

Work same as Cowl for 8 rows:
28 dc and 3 sc.

COWL

Ch 23.

Row 1: Sc in second ch from
hook and in next 2 chs, ★ ch 3,
skip next 2 chs, sc in next 5 chs;
repeat from ★ once **more**, ch 3,
skip next 2 chs, sc in last 3 chs:
16 sc and 3 ch-3 sps.

Row 2 (Right side)**:** Ch 1, turn; sc
in first sc, ★ 9 dc in next ch-3 sp,
skip next 2 sc, sc in next sc;
repeat from ★ 2 times **more**:
27 dc and 4 sc.

Note: Loop a short piece of
yarn around any stitch to mark
Row 2 as **right** side.

Row 3: Ch 4 **(counts as first dc plus ch 1)**, turn; skip next 2 dc, sc in next 5 dc, ★ ch 3, skip next 5 sts, sc in next 5 dc; repeat from ★ once **more**, ch 1, skip next 2 dc, dc in last sc: 17 sts and 4 sps.

Row 4: Ch 3 **(counts as first dc)**, turn; 4 dc in first dc, skip next 2 sc, sc in next sc, ★ 9 dc in next ch-3 sp, skip next 2 sc, sc in next sc; repeat from ★ once **more**, skip next 2 sc and last ch-1 sp, 5 dc in last dc: 28 dc and 3 sc.

Row 5: Ch 1, turn; sc in first 3 dc, ★ ch 3, skip next 5 sts, sc in next 5 dc; repeat from ★ once **more**, ch 3, skip next 5 sts, sc in last 3 dc: 16 sc and 3 ch-3 sps.

Row 6: Ch 1, turn; sc in first sc, ★ 9 dc in next ch-3 sp, skip next 2 sc, sc in next sc; repeat from ★ 2 times **more**: 27 dc and 4 sc.

Repeat Rows 3-6 for pattern until piece measures approximately 27" (68.5 cm) from beginning ch, ending by working Row 4.

Last Row: Ch 1, turn; sc in first 3 dc, ★ ch 2, skip next 5 sts, sc in next 5 dc; repeat from ★ once **more**, ch 2, skip next 5 sts, sc in last 3 dc: 16 sc and 3 ch-2 sps.

Trim: Ch 1, turn; 3 sc in first sc, sc in next 2 sc, 2 sc in next ch-2 sp, (sc in next 5 sc, 2 sc in next ch-2 sp) twice, sc in next 2 sc, 3 sc in last sc; sc evenly across ends of rows; working in free loops of beginning ch **(Fig. 3b, page 155)**, 3 sc in ch at base of first sc, sc in next 2 chs, 2 sc in next ch-2 sp, (sc in next 5 chs, 2 sc in next ch-2 sp) twice, sc in next 2 chs, 3 sc in last ch; sc evenly across ends of rows; join with slip st to first sc, finish off.

With **right** side facing and using photo as a guide for placement, sew one button at base of each 9-dc group on Row 2.

To wear your Cowl as shown, use ch-2 sps on last row as buttonholes.

To wear your Cowl as shown on page 144, use spaces formed at the side edge as buttonholes.

Messenger Bag

◼◼☐☐ EASY

DESIGNED BY
Kristi Simpson

Finished Measurements:

7¼" wide x 9" tall (18.5 cm x 23 cm)

SHOPPING LIST

- **Yarn** (Medium Weight) **4**
  [4 ounces, 200 yards
  (113 grams, 183 meters) per skein]:
  - 1 skein

- **Crochet Hook**
  - Size H (5 mm) **or** size needed
    for gauge

- **Additional Supplies**
  - Yarn needle
  - Sewing needle
  - Sewing thread
  - 1¼" (32 mm) buttons - 3

Gauge Information:

15 sc and 18 rows = 4" (10 cm)

Gauge Swatch:

4" (10 cm) square

Ch 16.

Row 1: Sc in second ch from hook and in each ch across: 15 sc.

Rows 2-18: Ch 1, turn; sc in each sc across.

Finish off.

STITCH GUIDE

SINGLE CROCHET 2 TOGETHER
(abbreviated sc2tog)

Pull up a loop in each of next 2 sc, YO and draw through all 3 loops on hook **(counts as one sc)**.

BODY

Ch 28.

Row 1 (Right side): Working in back ridge of beginning ch **(Fig. 2, page 155)**, sc in second ch from hook and in each ch across: 27 sc.

Note: Loop a short piece of yarn around any stitch to mark Row 1 as **right** side.

Rows 2-40: Ch 1, turn; sc in each sc across.

Row 41 (Turning ridge): Ch 1, turn; sc in Back Loop Only of each sc across **(Fig. 4, page 155)**.

Rows 42-87: Ch 1, turn; sc in both loops of each sc across; at end of Row 87, do **not** finish off.

Flap Shaping

Row 1 (Decrease row): Ch 1, turn; sc in first sc, sc2tog, sc in each sc across: 26 sc.

Row 2: Ch 1, turn; sc in each sc across.

Rows 3-26: Repeat Rows 1 and 2, 12 times: 14 sc.

Row 27 (Buttonhole row): Ch 1, turn; sc in first sc, sc2tog, sc in next 4 sc, ch 4 (buttonhole), skip next 4 sc, sc in last 3 sc: 9 sc and one ch-4 sp.

Row 28: Ch 1, turn; sc in first 3 sc, 4 sc in next ch-4 sp, sc in each sc across to last 2 sc, sc2tog: 12 sc.

Row 29: Ch 1, turn; sc in first sc, sc2tog, sc in each sc across: 11 sc.

Row 30: Ch 1, turn; sc in first 8 sc, sc2tog, leave last sc unworked: 9 sc.

Row 31: Ch 1, turn; sc in first sc, sc2tog, sc in last 6 sc; finish off.

STRAP

Leaving a long end for sewing, ch 196.

Row 1: Sc in back ridge of second ch from hook and each ch across: 195 sc.

Rows 2-4: Ch 1, turn; sc in each sc across.

Finish off leaving a long end for sewing.

FINISHING

With **wrong** side together, fold Body at turning ridge. Sew side seams.

Using long ends, sew approximately 1½" (4 cm) of each end of Strap to a side seam.

Sew lower button to Body to correspond with buttonhole; then sew remaining two buttons to Flap evenly spaced apart.

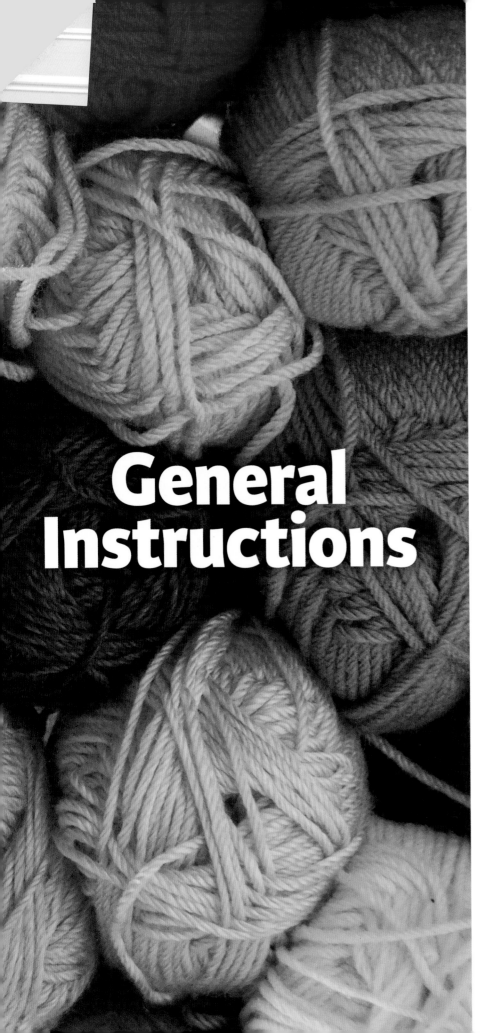

General Instructions

Abbreviations

BPdc	Back Post double crochet(s)
BPtr	Back Post treble crochet(s)
CC	Contrasting Color
ch(s)	chain(s)
cm	centimeters
dc	double crochet(s)
dc2tog	double crochet 2 together
ex sc	extended single crochet(s)
ex sc2tog	extended single crochet(s) 2 together
FP	Front Post
FPdc	Front Post double crochet(s)
FPdc2tog	Front Post double crochet 2 together
FPdtr	Front Post double treble crochet(s)
FPsc	Front Post single crochet(s)
fsc	foundation single crochet(s)
FPtr	Front Post treble crochet(s)
hdc	half double crochet(s)
hdc2tog	half double crochet 2 together
Ldc	Long double crochet(s)
MC	Main Color
mm	millimeters
Rnd(s)	Round(s)
sc	single crochet(s)
sc2tog	single crochet 2 together
sc3tog	single crochet 3 together
sp(s)	space(s)
st(s)	stitch(es)
tr	treble crochet(s)
YO	yarn over

Symbols & Charts

★ — work instructions following ★ as many **more** times as indicated in addition to the first time.

† to † — work all instructions from first † to second † as **many** times as specified.

( ) or **[ ]** — work enclosed instructions **as many** times as specified by the number immediately following **or** work all enclosed instructions in the stitch or space indicated **or** contains explanatory remarks.

colon (:) — the number(s) given after a colon at the end of a row or round denote(s) the number of stitches or spaces you should have on that row or round.

Gauge

Exact gauge is **essential** for proper size. Before beginning your project, make the sample swatch given in the individual instructions in the yarn or thread and hook specified. After completing the swatch, measure it, counting your stitches and rows or rounds carefully. If your swatch is larger or smaller than specified, **make another, changing hook size to get the correct gauge**. Keep trying until you find the size hook that will give you the specified gauge.

CROCHET TERMINOLOGY

United States		International
slip stitch (slip st)	=	single crochet (sc)
single crochet (sc)	=	double crochet (dc)
half double crochet (hdc)	=	half trebel crochet (htr)
double crochet (dc)	=	treble crochet (tr)
treble crochet (tr)	=	double treble crochet (dtr)
double treble crochet (dtr)	=	triple treble crochet (ttr)
triple treble crochet (tr tr)	=	quadruple treble crochet (qtr)
skip	=	miss

CROCHET HOOKS

United States	Metric (mm)	United States	Metric (mm)	United States	Metric (mm)
B-1	2.25	7	4.5	M/N-13	9
C-2	2.75	H-8	5	N/P-15	10
D-3	3.25	I-9	5.5	P/Q	15
E-4	3.5	J-10	6	Q	16
F-5	3.75	K-10½	6.5	S	19
G-6	4	L-11	8		

STEEL CROCHET HOOKS

United States	Metric (mm)	United States	Metric (mm)	United States	Metric (mm)
00	3.5	5	1.9	11	1.1
0	3.25	6	1.8	12	1
1	2.75	7	1.65	13	.85
2	2.25	8	1.5	14	.75
3	2.1	9	1.4		
4	2	10	1.3		

▰▱▱▱ **BASIC**		Projects using basic stitches. May include basic increases and decreases.
▰▰▱▱ **EASY**		Projects may include simple stitch patterns, color work, and/or shaping.
▰▰▰▱ **INTERMEDIATE**		Projects may include involved stitch patterns, color work, and/or shaping.
▰▰▰▰ **COMPLEX**		Projects may include complex stitch patterns, color work, and/or shaping using a variety of techniques and stitches simultaneously.

Yarn Weight Symbol & Names	LACE 0	SUPER FINE 1	FINE 2	LIGHT 3	MEDIUM 4	BULKY 5	SUPER BULKY 6	JUMBO 7
Type of Yarns in Category	Fingering, size 10 crochet thread	Sock, Fingering, Baby	Sport, Baby	DK, Light Worsted	Worsted, Afghan, Aran	Chunky, Craft, Rug	Super Bulky, Roving	Jumbo, Roving
Crochet Gauge* Ranges in Single Crochet to 4" (10 cm)	32-42 sts**	21-32 sts	16-20 sts	12-17 sts	11-14 sts	8-11 sts	6-9 sts	5 sts and fewer
Advised Hook Size Range	Steel*** 6 to 8, Regular hook B-1	B-1 to E-4	E-4 to 7	7 to I-9	I-9 to K-10½	K-10½ to M/N-13	M/N-13 to Q	Q and larger

*GUIDELINES ONLY: The chart above reflects the most commonly used gauges and hook sizes for specific yarn categories.

** Lace weight yarns are usually crocheted with larger hooks to create lacy openwork patterns. Accordingly, a gauge range is difficult to determine. Always follow the gauge stated in your pattern.

*** Steel crochet hooks are sized differently from regular hooks–the higher the number, the smaller the hook, which is the reverse of regular hook sizing.

Markers

Markers are used to help distinguish the beginning of each round being worked. Place a 2" (5 cm) scrap piece of yarn before the first stitch of each round, moving marker after each round is complete or when noted in instructions.

Markers are also used to mark placement of increases and decreases. Place a 2" (5 cm) scrap piece of yarn as indicated, moving them up as each round is worked.

Sizing

Gloves

Measure around the widest part of your hand, usually across the knuckles *(Fig. 1a)*. Glove sizing is based on this measurement, so pick a finished measurement approximately ½" to 1" (1.25 cm to 2.5 cm) smaller than your hand measurement to obtain a comfortable fit.

Fig. 1a

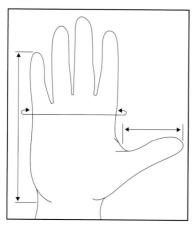

Hats

To determine what size to make, measure around the crown of your head with a tape measure *(Fig. 1b)*. As long as the Hat is made from a yarn with elasticity, the fabric will have some give. You want the band to fit snugly, so chose the size closest to your measurement or slightly smaller. You can also adjust the band size by changing the hook size used for it, and therefore adjusting the gauge and the finished measurement.

Fig. 1b

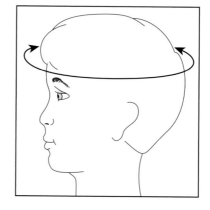

Joining with Sc

When instructed to join with sc, begin with a slip knot on hook. Insert hook in stitch or space indicated, YO and pull up a loop, YO and draw through both loops on hook.

Joining with Dc

When instructed to join with dc, begin with a slip knot on the hook. YO, holding loop on hook, insert hook in stitch or space indicated, YO and pull up a loop (3 loops on hook), (YO and draw through 2 loops on hook) twice.

Zeros

To consolidate the length of an involved pattern, zeros are sometimes used so that all sizes can be combined. For example, sc in first 0{1-0} sc means the first and last sizes would do nothing and the middle size would work one sc in first sc.

Foundation Single Crochet
(abbreviated fsc)

Ch 2, insert hook in second ch from hook, YO and pull up a loop, YO and draw through one loop on hook **(ch made)**, YO and draw through both loops on hook **(first fsc made)**, ★ insert hook in ch at base of last fsc made, YO and pull up a loop, YO and draw through one loop on hook **(ch made)**, YO and draw through both loops on hook **(fsc made)**; repeat from ★ for each additional fsc.

Back Ridge of Chain

Work only in loops indicated by arrows *(Fig. 2)*.

Fig. 2

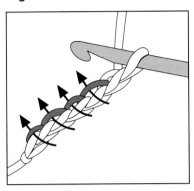

Free Loops

After working in Back or Front Loops Only on a row or round, there will be a ridge of unused loops. These are called the free loops. Later, when instructed to work in the free loops of the same row or round, work in these loops *(Fig. 3a)*.

When instructed to work in free loops of a chain, work in loop(s) indicated by arrow *(Fig. 3b or 3c)*.

Fig. 3a

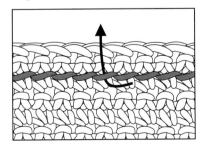

Fig. 3b

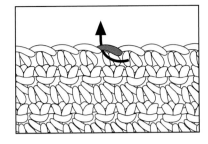

Fig. 3c

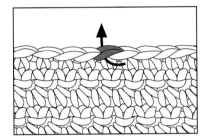

Back or Front Loops Only

Work only in loop(s) indicated by arrow *(Fig. 4)*.

Fig. 4

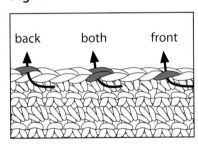

Changing Colors

Work the last stitch to within one step of completion, hook new yarn *(Figs. 5a-c)* and draw through both loops on hook.

To change colors at the end of a round, drop yarn, with new yarn, join with slip st to first st *(Fig. 5d)*. Cut old yarn and work over both ends, unless otherwise instructed.

Fig. 5a

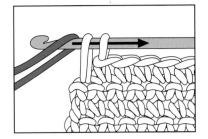

Fig. 5b

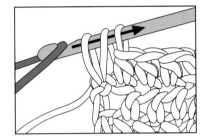

Fig. 5c

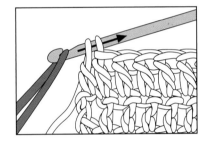

Fig. 5d

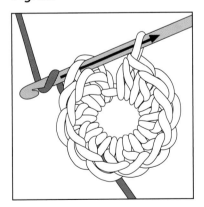

Post Stitch

Work around post of stitch indicated, inserting hook in direction of arrow *(Fig. 6)*.

Fig. 6

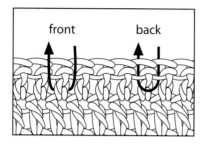

Working In Space Before A Stitch

When instructed to work in space before a stitch or in spaces between stitches, insert hook in space indicated by arrow *(Fig. 7)*.

Fig. 7

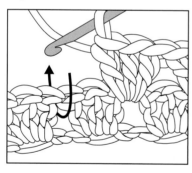

Weaving Through Stitches

Thread a yarn needle with the long end left at the end of the piece and weave it through the stitches on the last round worked *(Fig. 8)*.

Fig. 8

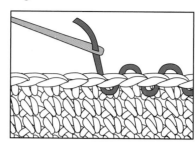

Reverse Single Crochet
(abbreviated reverse sc)

Working from **left** to **right**, ★ insert hook in stitch to right of hook *(Fig. 9a)*, YO and draw through, under and to left of loop on hook (2 loops on hook) *(Fig. 9b)*, YO and draw through both loops on hook *(Fig. 9c)* **(reverse sc made, *Fig. 9d*)**; repeat from ★ around.

Fig. 9a

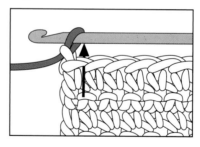

Fig. 9b

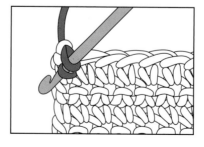

Fig. 9c

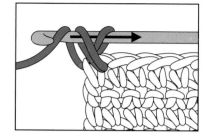

Fig. 9d

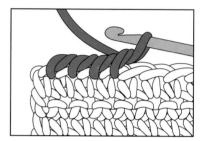

Fringe

Cut a piece of cardboard 6" (15 cm) wide and half as long as specified in individual instructions for strands. Wind the yarn **loosely** and **evenly** around the cardboard lengthwise until the card is filled, then cut across one end; repeat as needed.

Hold together as many strands of yarn as specified for the finished fringe; fold in half. With **wrong** side facing and using a crochet hook, draw the folded end up through a space or row and pull the loose ends through the folded end *(Fig. 10a)*; draw the knot up tightly *(Fig. 10b)*. Repeat spacing as desired.

Fig. 10a

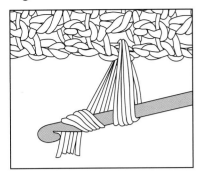

Fig. 10b

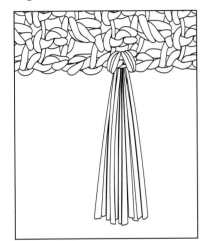

Fair Isle Techniques

Fair Isle is a technique used to create patterns with many colors. Only two colors are used on each round and the unused color is worked over, weaving it into the fabric.

Gauge While Changing Colors

For the stitches to look uniform and also for the project to match the finished size given in the instructions, it is essential to maintain stitch gauge while changing colors. You will also be assured that you have enough yarn to finish your project.

Changing Colors

To change colors in sc, insert the hook in the next sc, YO and pull up a loop (2 loops on hook); drop yarn to **wrong** side of work, with new color, YO and draw through both loops on hook **(Fig. 11a)**.

Fig. 11a

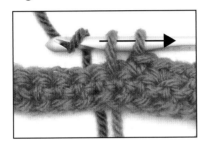

To join a new color with a slip st, insert the hook in the first st of the rnd. Pick up the color specified, YO with the new color and draw it through the st and the loop on the hook **(Fig. 11b)**.

Fig. 11b

This method gives the joining a smooth look **(Fig. 11c)**.

Fig. 11c

When it's time to change to a previously used color, hold the yarn **loosely** on the **wrong** side of the work while drawing it up to join with slip st **(Fig. 11d)**.

Fig. 11d

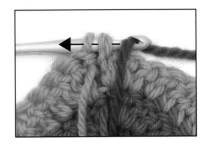

Always keep the first color used in a round above the second color as you change colors no matter which color you are changing to **(Fig. 11e)**.

Fig. 11e

Yarn Floats are created when a color is carried **loosely** on the **wrong** side of the work **(Fig. 11f)**.

Fig. 11f

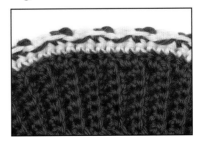

Work over the floats on the next round *(Fig. 11g)*, enclosing them within the fabric to prevent the yarn from showing on the front or back.

Fig. 11g

How To Follow A Chart

The chart shows each stitch as a square, indicating what color each stitch should be.

To keep your place, a ruler, piece of paper, or a sticky note can be placed **above** the round you are working. You need to see the round you have just completed to ensure you are working the correct color.

When working in rounds always follow each row of the chart from **right** to **left**.

Finishing Components

All components used in this book can be found in the beading/jewelry section of any craft store. Here are products similar to the ones we used.

Bails are attached to beads and other objects to create pendants. They come in many sizes, shapes, and designs.

Bead caps add texture and sparkle when placed next to beads.

Chains come in a variety of sizes, styles, color, and finishes.

Chandelier findings provide a base with bottom loops to which bead drops and other embellishments can be attached and a top loop for attaching an ear wire.

Clasps of all sizes, shapes, and styles are available. Lobster clasps are shaped like a lobster's claw and have a spring-action closure. A toggle clasp is secured by sliding the bar through the loop.

Just about any earring style can be made with the wide variety of ear wires available — fishhook and lever-back are used in this book.

A head pin is straight wire with a head of some sort; the ones used in this book are flat but there are several decorative styles as well.

Jump rings are metal round or oval rings that are used to attach jewelry components to each other. The rings are opened and closed with chain-nose pliers.

Tools

Chain-nose pliers have rounded, tapered jaws and a flat interior that will not mar wire or metal findings. These pliers are used for opening and closing jump rings and bending wire. You will need 2 pair to open jump rings and loops on head pins and ear wires.

Round-nose pliers have round jaws that are useful for making loops and bending wire smoothly.

Wire cutters are used to cut beading wire, head pins and other soft metals.

A flexible wire beading needle has a collapsible eye that allows it to go through small-hole beads and can be used to sew Motifs together.

Library of Congress Control Number: 2019937363

We have made every effort to ensure that these instructions are accurate and complete.
We cannot, however, be responsible for human error, typographical mistakes, or variations
in individual work.

Production Team: Instructional/Technical Editor—Linda A. Daley; Senior Graphic Artist—Lora Puls;
Graphic Artist—Michael Douglas; Photo Stylist—Lori Wenger; and Photographer—Jason Masters.

Made in China